Modern Management
and Leadership

Internal Audit and IT Audit

Series Editor:
Dan Swanson
Dan Swanson and Associates, Ltd.,
Winnipeg, Manitoba, Canada.

The Internal Audit and IT Audit series publishes leading-edge books on critical subjects facing audit executives as well as internal and IT audit practitioners. Key topics include Audit Leadership, Cybersecurity, Strategic Risk Management, Auditing Various IT Activities and Processes, Audit Management, and Operational Auditing.

Modern Management and Leadership

Best Practice Essentials with CISO/CSO Applications

Mark Tarallo

CRC Press
Taylor & Francis Group
Boca Raton London New York

CRC Press is an imprint of the
Taylor & Francis Group, an **informa** business

First edition published 2022
by CRC Press
6000 Broken Sound Parkway NW, Suite 300, Boca Raton, FL 33487-2742

and by CRC Press
2 Park Square, Milton Park, Abingdon, Oxon, OX14 4RN

ISBN: 9780367558918 (hbk)
ISBN: 9781032039794 (pbk)
ISBN: 9781003095620 (ebk)

Typeset in Adobe Caslon Pro
by codeMantra

For my father, an excellent executive-level manager, an excellent educational leader as a founding faculty business professor, and an even better man.

Contents

PART IV   LEADERS IN ACTION

PART V   THE FUTURE OF MANAGEMENT AND LEADERSHIP

Preface

From my very beginnings as a journalist 30-odd years ago, I have covered leaders in action. On a reporting fellowship in the Middle East which began my career, I covered the deadly shooting of an Iranian passenger jet by the U.S. Navy, and I followed how military and diplomatic leaders reacted to this shattering international crisis. As a newspaper political reporter, I spent 12-hour days covering state senators and representatives in the Virginia Legislature, the oldest continuous law-making body in the New World. I also covered the inauguration and early career of the first African-American U.S. governor ever elected.

As an international trade correspondent for a wire service, I covered global summit meetings featuring dozens of heads of state. Back in Washington, D.C., I covered leaders on Capitol Hill and from two presidential administrations. This included covering leaders in the crucible, during events like the 9/11 attacks, the WTO "Battle in Seattle" summit meeting, and the disputed U.S. presidential election of 2000.

But about a dozen years ago, the practice of management and leadership became one of my primary beats. I wrote about nearly every imaginable aspect of it. I conducted countless in-depth interviews with successful leaders and management experts. I covered management and leadership conference sessions and seminars. I researched management trends, seminal studies, and the evolution of management and leadership.

Eventually, it dawned on me: the accumulated best practice guidance, practical advice, and performance essentials I had gleaned from years of interviews, research, and reporting should be compiled in a book. I thought such a book could be a valuable resource for managers and leaders (be they aspiring or seasoned) open to learning. Call it kismet, but sometime later, a representative for CRC Press contacted me and asked if I had any book ideas.

Herewith. Hope it serves.

Acknowledgments

I have interviewed and gained knowledge, wisdom, and perspective from hundreds of experts, surely too many to list. But below are some experts whom I found particularly astute for the purposes of this book. I am grateful for their time and insight.

James Abruzzo, Head of Nonprofit Practice, DHR International; President, Abruzzo Associates

Art Barter, Founder and CEO, Servant Leadership Institute

Jordan Birnbaum, Chief Behavioral Economist, ADP

George Bradt, author of *Onboarding*, co-author of *The New Leader's 100-Day Action Plan*

Hart S. Brown, Senior Vice President, R3 Continuum

William Cottringer, Executive Vice President, PalAmerican Security/Cascade Security Corp.

Stephen M.R. Covey, former CEO of the Covey Leadership Center, author of *The Speed of Trust*

Sam Curry, CSO, Cybereason

Paula Davis, Founder and CEO of The Stress and Resilience Institute

Laura DiFlorio, Happiness Manager, Nobscot Corporation

McLean Essiene, President and CEO,
Essimacs International Security Ltd.

Pat Falotico, former CEO of the Robert K.
Greenleaf Center for Servant Leadership

Jim Harter, Chief Scientist of Workplace and Well-Being, Gallup

Phil Haussler, Head of Product, Quantum Workplace

Darlene Hunter, President and CEO,
Darlene Hunter and Associates LLC

Bob Kelleher, President and Founder,
The Employee Engagement Group

Brad Kieserman, Vice President of Disaster Operations
and Logistics, American Red Cross

Scott Klososky, futurist and Founder of Future Point of View

David Lammert, President, Pinnacle Placements

Tony Marzulli, Vice President for Talent Solutions, ADP

Desi Matel-Anderson, former Chief Innovation Advisor,
Federal Emergency Management Agency

Marie G. McIntyre, author of *The Management Team Handbook*

Peter Power, former Chairman of World Conference
on Disaster Management

Khalil Smith, former Head of Diversity and Inclusion Practice,
NeuroLeadership Institute

Jane Snipes, Managing Partner, Northstar Recruiting

Darryl Spivey, Senior Faculty Member,
Center for Creative Leadership

Chris Stuart, Vice President, Top Guard Security

Michael Timmes, Human Resource Consultant, Insperity

John Torres, President, Guidepost Solutions

Brady Wilson, co-founder of Juice Inc., author of *Beyond Engagement*

Caroline Wong, Chief Strategy Officer at Cobalt.io,
author of *Security Metrics*

About the Author

 **Mark Tarallo** is a multi-award-winning journalist and writer who has covered and analyzed management and leadership issues for more than two decades. He has interviewed and covered hundreds of leaders and managers from the private, public, and nonprofit sector, from CEOs and generals to senators and cabinet secretaries to association executives and security managers. He has been senior reporter for *CEO Update* magazine, and has covered management and leadership issues in the security space for *Security Management* magazine. He also served as international trade correspondent for a global wire service, where he covered global summit meetings such as the 1999 World Trade Organization ministerial meeting in Seattle and FTAA Summit of the Americas in Quebec City in 2001.

Mr. Tarallo has won more than 20 awards for his writing and reporting. His article "The Art of Servant Leadership" won the Award of Excellence in the 2018 APEX Awards for Publishing Excellence competition, and his analysis of failed leadership in the public sector, The "Lessons of Flint," won the Grand Award in Writing in the 2017 Apex competition. He earned a bachelor's degree from the University of California-Berkeley and a master's degree from the University of Texas at Austin. He can be reached by email at *modernmanagementandleadership@outlook.com*.

PART I

MANAGING AND LEADING: EVOLUTION/ REVOLUTION

1

THE FAILURE OF TRADITIONAL MANAGEMENT AND LEADERSHIP

"The Very Practice of Management No Longer Works."

These are the opening words of a rather formidable source: the most recent updated edition of Gallup's *State of the American Workplace* report, released in 2020. The report is one of the most comprehensive surveys of U.S. management trends and practices in existence. It is based on the fortress of data that Gallup maintains: nearly 200,000 employee participants in the company's various panels and polls, and more than 31 million survey respondents included in its client database.

The report contains some sobering statistics. A majority of employees – 51 percent – say they are not engaged at work. Only about one-third of employees say that they are engaged. A large majority of employees say that they are not managed in a way that motivates them to do outstanding work.

"These figures indicate an American leadership philosophy that simply doesn't work anymore," Gallup CEO Jim Clifton writes in the report.

In 2019, Gallup found a similar trend worldwide. Its *State of the Global Workplace* report found that global employee engagement was a dismal 15 percent.

"The current practice of management – which attempts to turn weaknesses into strengths – doesn't work," the report says of global management practices.

In sum, a majority of workers around the world are not engaged at a work. A large majority say that they are not managed in a way that motivates them to do outstanding work. The traditional leadership philosophy, and the current practice of management, does not work anymore.

This was the grim state of management when COVID-19 hit in early 2020. The coronavirus pandemic transformed the world and the workplace. The pandemic did not alleviate the negative trends that Gallup and many others were witnessing and experiencing in the management and leadership space.

It accelerated those trends. In the management and leadership space, the pandemic served as an accelerator. Needed changes to the practice of management and leadership are now needed even more.

So, if the Gallup findings are correct, and the very practice of current management and leadership no longer works, how can you buck the trend and be a superb manager and a stellar leader?

Read this book, and follow its guidance.

What the New Workforce Wants and Needs: Mission, Purpose, Meaning

"Of course, all employees need fair pay. But they are now driven more than ever by mission and purpose and require a workplace culture that delivers it," writes Clifton in the *Global Workplace* report.

That is what the workforce of the future will need and want: a workplace that delivers *mission* and *purpose*. To those two components, add a third to arrive at the Holy Trinity: work that is *meaningful*.

"Researchers have shown meaningfulness to be more important to employees than any other aspect of work, including pay and rewards, opportunities for promotion, or working conditions," write Catherine Bailey and Adrian Madden in the *MIT Sloan Management Review*.

What is meaningful work? Bailey and Madden found that meaning-fulness has some essential attributes. It matters to people other than just themselves, so it is self-transcendent. It often feels poignant and emotionally deep. It comes and goes in an episodic fashion. It is more often experienced in a reflective mode rather than in the moment. It is best understood within the context of one's personal life experiences.

But being aligned with mission, having a deep purpose, and accomplishing meaningful work are by no means a given in many jobs, professions, roles, and organizations. (Bailey and Madden, in their research, found that "poor management" was the top destroyer of meaningfulness.)

And so, workers in the new workforce need and want to work for managers and leaders who will understand and build on their strengths, give them developmental opportunities to fulfill their potential and career goals, recognize their accomplishments and contributions, and coach them in real time.

They need and want managers who serve as matchmakers of mission and meaning.

These leaders take the time and effort to understand and appreciate the capabilities of each individual team member, and then align them with the organization's mission to best make use of those talents. This alignment is successful when the employee feels they are putting in meaningful work that advances the organization's mission and gives the team member a sense of purpose.

Which Managers and Leaders Will Succeed?

Leaders and managers who serve as matchmakers of mission and meaning increase their chances of succeeding.

Leadership and management styles will vary, but most of them will share certain best practices. Similarly, the guidance and counsel offered in this book ranges widely but threaded throughout are core principles.

These successful leaders and managers will strive to reach a pro-found level of professional connection with their team members, through ongoing conversation. They will take the time to understand their employees' perspectives, their goals, their motivations, their individualized sense of purpose, and what is meaningful to them in their professional lives.

They will strive to sustain a humane workplace that makes the most out of the contributions by team members by identifying and developing skills and then capitalizing on them to the benefit of both the team member and the organization.

As strong communicators, these successful leaders and managers recognize and articulate. They recognize accomplishments and strong skill levels, and they articulate how the team member's work makes a vital contribution to the organization's mission, and how the staffer brings value to the organization.

They demonstrate, through example, that the relationship between leader and team member is a two-way street. They are close listeners; they seek and value the views, ideas, and perspectives of team members. They coach to strengths and help team members develop in a way that supports their career goals.

These leaders and managers have a dual mission: to best serve the organization they are helping to manage, and to best serve the people they are leading. And they do not take for granted their prominence in the eyes of those they lead and manage.

Reader, if you are a manager or leader, then by dint of your position as somebody's "boss," you are very likely one of the key figures in their life.

Consider, then, your position and influence. What you say can reverberate in an employee's head for days, weeks, months, and years. A negative comment can resurface – sometimes with ruining effect. This can happen to a team member during vacations, during cherished time spent with family and friends, during otherwise restorative downtime.

Keep this in mind. Successful leaders and managers usually do.

Interlude: Note on the Text

The aim of this book is to help you consistently perform at the highest level as a manager, and fulfill your potential as a leader, as you move forward in this rapidly changing environment in the emerging post-COVID world, where many traditional management and leadership practices have been falling short.

The book is designed to guide leaders and managers, both aspiring and seasoned, at any stage of their careers.

Many workers first become a manager when they are promoted into a managerial role on the basis of their performance in their previous non-managerial job. But no one gives them practical advice and best practice guidance on actual tasks they will have to manage, such as hiring and onboarding and coaching, keeping team members engaged and inspired, sustaining a healthy workplace culture, mitigating bias, and turning around difficult employees.

This book does that. It will also help seasoned managers take their performance up to the next level, and help them make adjustments to ensure their practices stay relevant moving forward.

Part III, on leadership, offers guidance and best practices for a range of different leadership modes. It takes this approach because most successful leaders are actually many leaders in one: a two-way leader, a crisis leader, a service leader, a sustaining leader, etc. The chapters offer advice on how to lead in whatever mode you need to be in.

Part IV offers brief in-the-trenches case studies from successful managers and leaders, CISOs and CSOs, in different situations, and in locations ranging from Silicon Valley to West Africa.

Part V concludes this book with a brief look at leading in the future.

Enjoy!

PART II
Best Practices for Every Management Role

2

CRUCIAL EARLY DAYS:
EFFECTIVE ONBOARDING

Picture this. It is the first day on the job for your latest hire. Your new employee is eager and energetic, buzzing around the office with an easy smile for all, radiating enthusiasm.

Fast forward a few months. The new hire seems chastened and diminished, schlumping around the office like a half-deflated balloon, radiating regret. An early exit from a job once considered a great career move may be imminent.

The likelihood of this disheartening scenario can be minimized with careful management of a strategic onboarding program.

The Fragile New

Onboarding, also known as organizational socialization, is the process through which new hires learn attitudes, knowledge, skills, and behaviors required to function effectively in their organizations, according to a definition included in a Society for Human Resource Management (SHRM) Foundation report, *Onboarding New Employees: Maximizing Success.*

Research and conventional wisdom both suggest that employees often have about three months to prove themselves in a new job, according to the report author Talya Bauer, an onboarding expert and university management professor.

However, new hires are physiologically vulnerable during this period.

This can be explained as follows. When undertaking familiar tasks, people often switch to autopilot to conserve energy and save brain power for other tasks that require more conscious thought. To imagine this, think of a driver on a daily commute to work. The familiarity of this task allows the driver to switch into mental autopilot mode; once he or she arrives, the person may have little or no recollection of the trip itself.

New hires have fewer autopilot opportunities; most actions in a new position require conscious thought. This is true even for remote workers who may have to get accustomed to new videoconference meetings, new contact patterns, and new online tasks. This creates "new hire fatigue," and it can make new hires less resilient. Thus, the mindset of new hires, who might be outwardly enthusiastic, can often be anxious and nervous, feeling confused and a bit lost.

In that mindset, when things don't go according to expectations, there's a greater chance for either a quick quit within the first 90 days or an exit for another opportunity within the first year. Roughly 46 percent of newly hired employees fail within 18 months, while only 19 percent achieve unequivocal success, according to a study conducted by business consulting firm Leadership IQ.

Strategically managed onboarding takes into consideration this fragile mindset. An effective onboarding program is crucial for achieving high levels of staff engagement, satisfaction, and retention. Yet, despite the stakes at play, many managers view onboarding as an afterthought.

Some merely spend the occasional hour or so explaining processes and policies, under the mistaken belief that this brief effort discharges them of their responsibilities. Such passive onboarding programs, which may include a brief one-time explanation of procedures and a checklist of disconnected tasks, are still common among many organizations.

A Strategic Program

As a manager, think of onboarding not as a passive rote process but as a strategic program, as a process that begins during the recruiting phase, before the prospective new team member is even hired.

During the interview process, make sure that the candidate is given information about the culture of the organization and is encouraged to do due diligence on what it would be like to work there. Framing the culture in a positive way is acceptable, but the overall presentation should be truthful, not an oversell.

Once a new hire accepts an offer, ensure that existing staffers are in alignment before the new employee's first day. Team members should know what the new hire's role will be, and how they should coordinate and work with the new employee. This important practice can minimize early resignations that sometimes result from conflicts with other staffers over who should do what.

Another key pre-day-one practice: logistical preparations. On day one, the new hire's workstation and computer should be ready, key cards and security clearances already arranged, and parking and other day-to-day necessities taken care of.

The positive benefits here are several. It helps avoid potentially demoralizing and bad-first-impression snafus such as a new hire arriving with no office or desk to sit at. It also allows your organization to demonstrate its competence and its caring from the start. Small gestures can go a long way in building on this impression: a *Welcome* sign hanging on the new hire's computer; a few balloons and colorful balls on the chair; a brand new mug or other small piece of company swag on the desk.

Establishing Foundational Premises

From day one, your guiding onboarding principle should be: go beyond compliance and cultivate connection.

By necessity, the early days of a new hire are often loaded with tasks such as completing forms, meeting new colleagues and management, HR orientation, becoming familiar with all relevant technologies, and starting on an initial assignment to hit the ground running.

In addition, employees are often briefed on the details of the job and expectations, as well as company rules and regulations.

However, these should not be the only tasks for the new hire. From day one, the new team member should be learning about the organization's mission, its positive impact, and the valuable contribution that he or she will be making toward that mission and impact.

This can be done in several ways. Some organizations prepare materials to support this effort. The U.S. Government Accountability Office (GAO), one of the largest auditing bodies in the world, used to screen an in-house film that illustrated the accomplishments of the agency.

In general, film or video can be a helpful tool in this regard, as long as it steers far clear of seeming like a propaganda reel, or a shoddy YouTube home video, or an infomercial reeking of hucksterism. A printed brief, easily read and well presented with photos and graphics, can also be helpful. Some organizations find that an orientation session helps to serve this purpose.

But overall, the mediums involved in the onboarding process are less important than the key message: Here is the positive contributions that the organization makes, the things of value that it does. Here is how you will help create this value. These concepts should be part of the running conversation that the new hire has with you and all other relevant staffers during the onboarding process.

Moreover, as a manager, you should encourage the new hire to increasingly make that running conversation a two-way one. For example, with a working knowledge of their resume, you might want to ask if their previous work experiences touched on some of the areas that the organization is now focused on. Even if not, natural transitions from previous experiences can be briefly discussed, and you may want to solicit the new employee's initial impressions and ideas about the working details of the organization's mission.

This type of discussion helps establish a foundational premise: the relationship forming between the new team member and the organization is a two-way one, in which the new staffer's ideas are valued.

At a recent SHRM annual conference, an onboarding expert joked that, when a new hire is asked "How's the new job?" by family and friends, they might reply with, "It's a dream come true – I filled out forms!"

As a manager, one of your goals should be to change the new hire's response in that situation to something along the lines of: "You know, it's a really interesting organization. They seem to be doing a lot of good things, like X and Y and Z..."

Acculturalization and Socialization

Certainly, an onboarding program is influenced by the resources that can be devoted to it. For example, on one end of this spectrum might be the "L'Oreal Fit," the shorter name for the L'Oreal company's onboarding program, Follow-Up and Integration Track (FIT).

The program lasts 18–24 months and is a multipart integration program that includes personalized meeting programs, training, roundtable discussions, and field experiences, such as site visits and shadowing programs. While many organizations might not have the budget or staffing to conduct a two-year program like L'Oreal's, an effective onboarding program can still be run with modest means if certain key concepts are followed.

Part of the process of facilitating a new connection involves conveying key components of the organization's culture, such as its values, its mores, and formal and informal organizational norms. This type of acculturation is critical; embedded in any culture are unconscious and unspoken beliefs that determine how things are done within the company. Failing to communicate this information often makes it more difficult for new employees to succeed, and can make them feel discouraged, or even ostracized.

This acculturation is also part of the socialization process. The new hire moves from feeling like an outsider to connecting with, and to some extent identifying with, the organization. Once the connection is established, the new employee is less likely to leave the organization prematurely. Some say evidence of the burgeoning connection can be heard in the language of new hires; they switch from referring to staff in terms of "you" ("do you guys like to do informal group lunches?") and move to the more self-inclusive "we" ("are we supposed to save small receipts on work travel?").

Research has found that acceptance into a work team strongly influences the employee commitment level and turnover rate. Often, a manager can facilitate the new hire's social comfort in the organization by briefing existing organizational staffers on how they can enhance the adjustment process for a new hire.

There are several ways to increase the chances of successful socialization. One is setting up an informal mentoring or "buddy" system that connects new employees with a more senior person (or persons) in a similar role who can help acclimate them.

This arrangement can be especially effective if the mentor is adept at discussing "between-the-lines" customs and practices within the organization. For example, just one of many possible topics here is how staffers interpret the company dress code. Knowledge and feedback such as this may help a new employee avoid awkward missteps. On a related point, you should be careful to "walk the talk" of your culture; frequently bypassing security checkpoints when you come into the office is not the behavior you want to model.

In addition to transferring cultural knowledge, managers and mentors should make an effort, even a relatively subtle one, to help carve out space in the culture for the new hire. This is especially important if the organization has many longtime employees who tend to dominate the workplace, which wittingly or unwittingly sets up a "this is us – love us or leave us" dynamic.

For example, if the hire is comfortable sharing personal interests (music, sports, arts, travel), introductions to other staff with the same interests can be helpful. And if the hire is comfortable discussing his or her cultural background, and that background is different from most of existing staff, the message should be an optimistic and inclusive one – that greater diversity will help make the collective staff stronger and more effective.

Another advisable practice is to arrange for the new hire to have frequent check-ins, not only with you but with your supervisor or the department head. Frequent brief conversations help reduce miscommunication and anxiety, and can help keep the new hire on track.

During these check-ins, the new team member's impressions and questions should be solicited and followed-up on when appropriate; this demonstrates from the beginning an active listening approach that is crucial for the effective management. These conversations are also a good time for a wellness check-in – the fragile mindset concept elucidated above can be discussed, which may be reassuring to new hires who are experiencing fatigue or exhaustion.

To facilitate new relationships, consider setting up networking opportunities for your new team member, both internally and externally. This can be particularly important if you are the manager of a security-related department, and your staffers are perceived as the "company police" who are neither socially nor culturally well integrated. If your department sometimes feel like the unloved stepchild of the organization, new blood and the new relationships that the new hire may form could be the catalyst for a more integrated department.

To help build bridges, consider onboarding program components such as a cross-divisional mentoring programs and training activities. Encouraging participation in companywide online community groups and message boards can also help break down silos and facilitate connections with employees from different departments of the organization.

Focal Points

Besides successful socialization, there are a few other goals for your new hire that may serve as guiding principles for your onboarding program.

One is role clarity. Everyone may suffer if expectations are ambiguous. Work on making the position as well defined as possible, and make the effort to help new hires understand their role and responsibilities. This may take several conversations. Although the role should be clear, be open to tweaks that benefit both the team member and the mission. Help all those involved avoid role conflict between new and existing employees.

Another is self-efficacy in job performance. An employee's feeling of self-efficacy may strongly influence his or her job satisfaction, commitment, and length of tenure. As a manager, take steps that will help boost the confidence of new hires as they navigate their new position. Always being open to questions and clarifications can be a big help in the job learning process. Positive feedback for even small accomplishments can also help. For example, open and clear acknowledgment of employee progress after the first few weeks can make the new hire more confident in tackling new assignments.

Another is knowledge of and fit within the organization's culture. Understanding the company's mission, goals, and values, as well as learning the firm's unique language and communications style, are key indicators of employee adjustment. As a manager, you can lead the effort to make the company's culture transparent, and help the new hire understand how he or she brings value to the culture and the organization at large.

A good way for you to reinforce these guiding principles is to collaborate with the new hire on an individual plan for performance and growth. As part of this plan, you can identify the skills the employee brings with them, as well as promising areas for development. Your new hire employee can be encouraged to draft up their own training plan for coming up to speed and implementing new skills.

A good closing note for successful strategic onboarding: don't overwhelm new hires. Allow for downtime for conversations, to complete new assignments at a comfortable pace, and to process new information and responsibilities. An occasional long lunch with team members may help everyone's morale.

3

MANAGING PARTNERSHIP: EMPLOYEE RETENTION AND ENGAGEMENT

More than 75 percent of employees who quit could have been retained by their employers. That's a primary finding from the Work Institute's *2020 Retention Report*, a study based on data from over 233,000 employees in the United States.

And the primary point, for the purposes of this chapter, is that the manager has enormous influence on a staffer's decision to stay or leave. The odds of deciding to leave decrease by 31 percent for every 1-point increase in the core driver ratings for supervisor, according to the study.

Failure to retain staffers is also costly. The cost of replacing an individual employee can range from one-half to two times the employee's annual salary, the Gallup company recently estimated.

For most of 2020 and spilling into 2021, the coronavirus pandemic upended labor markets. But before COVID hit, many labor markets were tight. In the United States, the U.S. Labor Department announced that in 2018, for the first time on record, jobs outnumbered job seekers. Such labor shortage conditions could return to many countries fairly quickly, giving many employees several alternative job options if they are interested in leaving.

Employees leave for various reasons. According to the Retention Report, the three top specific reasons for employees to leave jobs in 2019 were career development, work-life balance, and manager behavior. All three reasons fall under one broad umbrella of why employees leave companies: their employer is not meeting their expectations and needs.

As a manager, you can strengthen your retention efforts and retain more staffers by focusing more on the needs and expectations of team members. Best practice guidance on how to do this follows.

Onboarding Process Crucial

Successful retention efforts start on day one. For new staffers, this makes the onboarding process crucial – indeed, it sometimes serves as predictor as to whether the employee will be short term or long term.

Most team members want to feel a connection to their jobs, to their colleagues, and to their organizations. Through productive onboarding, the beginnings of those connections can be established early in the staffer's tenure.

As a manager, there are three goals to strive for during onboarding: the new staffer will learn what makes the company unique, will learn the mission and values of the company, and will learn how his or her job helps fulfill the mission of the organization.

To help accomplish this, make sure that the onboarding process is a two-way one. You should communicate the organization's accomplishments and story to new employees, but also focus on the new team member by communicating how his or her skill sets and work accomplishments will help the firm.

This latter focus on the new employee is crucial, and it is where many organizations fail. Companies may be adept at telling their own story, but a sole focus on the organization can leave the new employee feeling left out.

This can be an especially costly mistake with Millennials; work-place specialists say members of that generation want to be recognized. To avoid this mistake, make time early in the onboarding process to sit down with new employees to discuss their background and previous experiences, and how those may fit in to their current job and the organization's mission. Facilitating these early connections to the larger good helps ensure that the team member knows that their work matters.

To take this practice even further, as a manager you may also sit down with a new staffer and draft a sample career path, based on the employee's future goals. You can supplement this career path exercise by relating examples of former employees who held the same position as the new employee and went on to have a successful career.

It also helps to give new team members meaningful work as early as possible, which shows trust in their abilities and engages them from the start. And instead of relying on organizational charts to explain workflow and reporting structures, it helps to explain the unwritten rules and process quirks regarding how things work.

In addition, try to ensure that other onboarding practices are not inadvertently working against retention efforts. In some organizations, orientation sessions can devolve into hours of company policy and benefit information discussed in excruciating detail. Besides being boring, this can make the new workplace seem impersonal, and make the new employee feel like a cog in a giant wheel. Instead, use online or printed materials to communicate granular policy details, and focus on overviews during in-person meetings.

Finally, do not assume that what worked for you when you were hired will work for all new employees. Some new employees prefer a more hands-off "sink-or-swim" onboarding approach, while others like to be more actively guided, so discuss this with the new staffer and then tailor your approach appropriately.

Needs and Expectations

Once the tone is set during onboarding, the manager should continue to focus on the employee's needs and expectations to maximize the firm's chances of retaining the employee.

However, these needs and expectations change across the lifecycle of the employee. At three weeks, they are different from what they will be at three years.

Moreover, workers from different generations sometimes have different needs, experts say. In many cases, older Gen X employees are often driven by stability and financial security. Many Millennials are interested in the organization's approach to social responsibility, while also being focused on their developing career path. Finding the right balance to fulfill each of these motivations is key to maintaining a successful culture that meets the expectations and needs of team members.

However, exactly what constitutes a company's culture can be hard to define. In general, a company's culture is created through experiences that employees have with peers, managers, and executives. Maintaining a positive employee experience is usually an effective retention strategy. One way to help ensure that positivity is to maintain a humane workplace.

What is a humane workplace? First, it is one where coworkers have positive and productive relationships with each other. Second, it allows for work-life balance. Team members are not overwhelmed by work; they stay connected with life outside of work. Job responsibilities offer enough flexibility for opportunities to disconnect and recharge.

Remember, even meaningful work can become too all-consuming, and this can work against retention efforts because the staffer may look for a position that offers more time for a rich life outside of work.

Third, a humane workplace makes the most of contributions by team members. To retain talent, an organization has to identify and capitalize on the skills of its talent. Managers can support this by careful efforts to find out where employees' abilities are especially strong, and then make good use of them.

However, sometimes managers fail to do this because they are fixated on improving what they consider to be the weaknesses of the employee. Traditionally, many managers have developed talent by focusing on areas that need improvement, while areas of strength remained largely untouched. But it is much better for motivation and retention for a manager to articulate the employee's strong skill sets, and show that they are valued by making proper use of them.

Getting to the Heart of Retention

As a manager, you may find that a very useful open-ended question to ask a team member is: "What keeps you with this organization?" A honest discussion on this topic will reveal what is important to a staffer, be it compensation, colleagues, benefits, the workplace, or other factors.

Another key factor in effective retention is opportunity. Employees need opportunities to grow as professionals and opportunities to advance their career. So as a manager, think of yourself as a career developer. Try to help support the career goals of team members by assigning them to strategic projects or assignments that give them opportunities to develop and showcase their ideas via new platforms.

Remember that effective employee retention strategies must be built on an accurate knowledge and understanding of the interests and needs of staff. This accuracy is compromised when the organization places hard limits on how team members can express their ideas, preferences, and expectations.

Instead, organizations should ask for feedback in a way that brings out the truth. Go beyond rating aspects of jobs and workplaces on a numerical scale. Have discussions with team members about why they rate the way they do, what improvements they would like to see, what is important to them, and more.

In sum, managers and organizations should know why their employees join, why their employees stay, and why their employees leave.

Engagement

Low employee engagement is an oft-cited reason for an organization's high turnover rate. Sadly, poor engagement with one's job is a common condition, studies have found.

In late 2020, a Gallup Company survey found that only 36 percent of American employees were engaged – meaning they were highly involved in and committed to their work and workplace. That leaves almost two-thirds of U.S. workers who are not engaged. Moreover, 13 percent said they were actively disengaged – basically, unhappy at work, and potentially spreading unhappiness to colleagues.

Gallup researchers also found that organizations which sustain high employee engagement reap serious benefits on average, including higher profitability and productivity, lower absenteeism, and fewer staff safety incidents.

There are several best practices that organizations and managers can follow to maximize employee engagement. Think of the organization–team member relationship as a partnership. The organization is helping the team member reach his or her potential, while the team member's work is helping the organization reach its potential.

When this win–win partnership is working, the team member is more likely to happily put in discretionary effort, which often does wonders for the organization and workplace. That discretionary effort from the staffer usually comes naturally, because of the positive energy generated by simply being engaged.

Similar to retention, engagement strategies should begin early, at the hiring stage. Research has shown that an employee-employer values alignment at hiring leads to greater engagement. Thus, to have an engaged team, your organization should ensure that it is recruiting the right talent, whose values match the firm's.

Bob Kelleher, an expert who runs The Employee Engagement Group consultancy, illustrates this by using the acronym BEST. Employers tend to hire for the middle two letters, education (E) and skills (S), in hopes that they will be the most reflective of performance. But it is the first and last letters, behaviors (B) and traits (T), that best reflect employees' values.

Thus, employers should also focus on behaviors and traits in the hiring process, since a value alignment is key to engagement. Sometimes, disengagement is the result of the fact that the values of the company and the employee were never a match.

Values are crucial, in part, because high salaries are often not enough to ensure high engagement. Motivation comes from the heart; extrinsic motivators like competitive pay and benefits often fall far short of pursuing one's passion and values.

Gallup, which has long studied engagement and the U.S. workplace, has found that three factors stand out when it comes to increasing employee engagement: promoting and hiring the right managers;

focusing on building employee strengths; and a sustained two-way coaching dialogue between managers and team members.

The last two factors – which are also key for employee retention, as mentioned above – are effective in part because they are being driven from below, Gallup researchers found. Younger workers, such as members of the Millennial generation, often prefer a coach type of manager who focuses on strengths-based development. In a strengths-based workplace culture, employees often produce better work and are more engaged.

In its research, Gallup found that 67 percent of employees who say that their manager focuses on their strengths are engaged, compared with only 31 percent of the employees who say that their manager focuses on their weaknesses.

Leading Pro-engagement Policy Changes

As a manager, you may also have an opportunity within your organization to lead or assist an effort to change policies that would have a positive effect on employee engagement.

For example, your organization may want to consider reworking its performance review process so that engagement is discussed during reviews. These should be two-way, safe-space conversations, in which team members are comfortable talking about when they feel disengaged, for what reasons, and what could be done differently.

Such a change can help frame performance conversations as a way to look forward and help team members grow, not as a backward-looking "ways I disappointed my manager this year" review. Moreover, the annual review process can be changed from "performance appraisals" to "employee development planning conferences."

Another option is to explore the practice that some successful organizations have adopted of conducting informal "stay" interviews with staff. Instead of an exit interview, in which managers try to find out why employees are leaving, managers conducting stay interviews try to find out what it would take for an employee to stay.

Finally, workforce demographic may also drive an increased emphasis on employee engagement.

Millennials continue to increase their share of the global workforce. According to demographic estimates, members of the Millennial generation will comprise the majority of the global workforce from 2020 until at least 2030.

Experts say Millennials are keen on being engaged with their work, and want to feel their work has a purpose and is a positive reflection on their values. Studies show, for example, that recent MBAs with high earning power will work for a significantly lower salary if they truly believe in their jobs.

Will this generation transform the workplace and drive up employee engagement? Stay tuned, managers.

4

DANCING WITH MYSELF: SELF-MANAGEMENT AND BIAS MITIGATION

Confidence and competence are not correlated. Many managers think they are good managers; for some of them, reality has shown otherwise.

Why is there no confidence–competence correlation? Several studies have found an answer: there is a distinct human tendency to overrate one's own abilities and performance. Take, for example, an oft-cited survey in which 80 percent of respondents rated themselves as better-than-average drivers – a mathematical impossibility. Humans can be overconfident in many areas and not adept at self-assessing.

Self-knowledge requires great effort to attain, and achieving it can be no easy task. The results, however, will be worth it. Making this attempt to know thyself as a manager allows managers to maximize their strengths, minimize their shortcomings, and modify their responses and behaviors, all for the cause of becoming a more effective leader.

In short, achieving a certain level of self-knowledge allows managers to effectively self-manage. This is key because you can't manage others if you can't manage yourself.

Strengths Analysis

"History's great achievers – a Napoleon, a da Vinci, a Mozart – have always managed themselves. That, in large measure, is what makes them great achievers," writes Peter Drucker in his landmark book *Management Challenges of the 21st Century*. Drucker is considered one of the fathers of modern management; he developed one of the first executive MBA programs in the United States in the early 1970s.

Drucker's book is one of the few seminal works on self-management for managers, and it seems to have grown more relevant as the emphasis on values-based leadership has become more pronounced. Drucker advises managers to answer a series of questions about themselves, and then offers best practice guidance in each area: *What are my strengths? How do I perform? What are my values? Where do I belong? What can I contribute?*

Below is some practical guidance for self-analysis in each of these areas.

What Are My Strengths?

To gain more self-knowledge about your strengths, try a feedback analysis. Here is the method: after every key decision or key action you make, write down what you then expect will happen. A year later, compare these recorded expectations with the actual results.

Within a few years, you should have a clearer picture of where your strengths lie. Moreover, the analysis should also reveal what you are doing (or not doing) that deprives you from the benefits of your strengths.

For example, let's say as a manager you create a new operational plan for your department, and then write down your expectation that the plan will be implemented in a year. A year later, if there is no progress, the analysis may be indicating that your advocacy and people skills were insufficient to make the plan a reality.

This type of analysis can be important if you aspire to advance up the ranks of an organization. In some organizations, success in executive and upper management positions hinges on two skill sets: managing people and high-level strategy. But if you were promoted to your position based on their day-to-day technical mastery and performance, high-level strategy and people skills may not be your long suits. In that case, it may be wise to seek proper training.

How Do I Perform?

Different people perform differently, and many do not possess the self-knowledge to know how they get things done. To ascertain this about yourself, ask yourself a few questions.

Am I a reader or a listener? Unlike readers, listeners process information best through their ears. Successful leaders of large active groups, who retain and distill nearly everything they are told, are often listeners. Often they are auditory learners, and books on tape are a good resource for them. Readers process and retain information through reading.

How do I learn? Some learn only by doing. Some learn by writing or notetaking; the act of putting an idea on paper is a great help to their understanding of it, and it often helps them remember it. Others learn by hearing themselves talk: a senior leader may hold a meeting and talk at staff for a long time, which helps the leader process ideas. The principle for this latter example is similar to someone in therapy who learns a lot, and sometimes has insights and realizations, when hearing themselves articulate something to a therapist.

Effective leaders usually know the preferred learning and performing style of their team members, so they can help give them what they need to succeed. Similarly, coworkers should know the learning styles and performance modes of their coworkers. And team members should observe their managers, find out how they learn and perform, and adapt their methods to what will make the manager most effective.

What Are My Values?

To be effective in an organization, a manager's values must be compatible with the organization's values. They do not need to be exactly the same, but they must be close enough to coexist and not be in direct conflict.

Organizations show their true values in their daily operations. A company may say in its mission statement that "our people are our most important assets," but if that firm is doing little to address its problems of high turnover and bad working conditions, it is obviously not living its values.

For a new manager, the interview process is a good time to touch on these issues. For example, say that your values as a manager include a commitment to ethical conduct and work that makes a positive difference and helps develop team members. With this in mind, during your interview, you can discuss your approach to the new opportunity in terms of your values. You can make clear that you firmly believe in continual professional development for staff, and then ask about the possibility of providing workplace training programs and continuing education opportunities.

Where Do I Belong?

Managers should ask themselves: do I work well with people or do I work best alone? Some managers derive energy from interacting with people. Others love working in a team environment, but also like spending stretches of time alone, in a more solitary executive position, to devote to projects, policy, and strategy. Some enjoy toggling back and forth between solitude and company, but in an uneven split, such as spending 75 percent of work time alone and 25 percent with others.

Also ask yourself the president-versus-vice-president issue: Do I best perform as a decision maker or as an adviser? Some managers perform swimmingly as advisers but cannot take the burden and pressure of making final decisions. As a result, sometimes the manager-adviser fails if promoted to the number one position. Other managers can succeed as the top decision-maker if they have an adviser to force them to think and see different ramifications, so they can make decisions with self-confidence and courage.

How Can I Contribute?

Finally, managers should ask themselves: What should my contribution be? This question ties together different aspects of self-management: Given my strengths, my top-performing mode, my values, and my best environment, how can I make the greatest contribution to what needs to be done? For current managers, that question should come in tandem with workplace questions: What does the situation require? What results need to be achieved to make a difference?

The answers to these questions will differ, depending on the manager and the job in question. However, the following benchmark question can be helpful in many situations: Where and how can I achieve results that will make a difference within the next year and a half?

The results should be ambitious, but within reason. They should also be meaningful and make a difference. Ideally, they should also be visible and measurable.

Bias Mitigation

Examining yourself in the context of the abovementioned questions is a wise investment of time and effort, which will pay valuable dividends in the form of self-knowledge. Now it is time for you, as a manager, to confront another reality: You are biased.

That is not to say you are discriminatory or prejudiced. It is just to say that all humans have bias. Even the most effectively self-managed leaders are biased. We see the world through filters, and in general, we are not aware of those filters.

Bias can have a large impact on a manager's decisions, from hiring to assignments to performance reviews. This has made bias an important area of study for management scholars, with a traditional focus on what managers can do to reduce their own bias.

But scholars have found that reducing one's own bias is often too difficult to do effectively. Overcoming bias is not simply a matter of will. Managers who are determined and motivated to self-examine for bias are still likely to conclude that they are not significantly biased.

Instead, experts say it is more effective to try to mitigate bias by building procedures designed to weed out bias into operational systems. To illustrate, think of a stock investment algorithm that is based on a mathematical performance evaluation formula. The formula, based on hard data, serves as a way to avoid simply choosing stocks by one's gut feeling, which reflects personal bias.

Similarity Bias

For managers, one of the most relevant types of bias is similarity bias. Similarity bias represents the following feeling: people like me are better than others. The "people like me" similarities may range from ethnic background, religion, race, hobbies, and economic class to professional approach and personality types. Studies have found that this similarity bias can have a major impact on hiring decisions.

But similarity bias can affect more than just hiring. Promotions, succession plans, contractor awards, and assignment delegation are all vulnerable to similarity bias. It can also affect how you as a manager engage with others in meetings – i.e., listening to ideas from those you are favorable biased toward a little more intently than to ideas from others. Or you might review someone more favorably due to bias.

Of course, some try to use similarity bias in their favor, for career advancement purposes. Think of the staffer who learns to golf to bond with a golf-loving manager, or the interviewee who is coached to consciously mirror the interviewer's body language.

Given its potential impact, similarity bias must be contended with, and it is often most effective to do this proactively. First, you should be in the right mindset – accept bias as a natural condition of being human, without denying it. Second, decide which type of similarity bias you want to examine, and in what context. For example, similarity bias may be personal background, and the context may be the hiring pool you are looking at to fill a new position.

Then comes the mitigation effort. This entails examining candidates in the hiring pool and looking for similarities to yourself, such as similar educational credentials, similar economic/racial/geographic background, similar life experiences, and more.

Be mindful of these similarities when you are considering candidates. In your considerations, are you giving an edge to a candidate who went to the same university as you did, or grew up near you, or played the same sport in high school? In reality, these similarities may say nothing about their readiness for the new position, or their potential. Being mindful of this possibility of bias can put the candidates on a more level playing field.

Another mitigation method for similarity bias is the reframing of key questions. For example, in the hiring process, many organizations look for hires that will be a good "cultural fit" and enjoyable to work with on a day-to-day basis. Sometimes, the hiring manager frames this by using what is called the airplane test – if you are sitting next to this person on an airplane and forced to chat for three hours, would you enjoy it?

But to mitigate similarity bias, you as a manager can reframe this hiring question too: if the plane went down and we had to work in tandem, which candidate would most enhance our chances of survival? In the long run, teams with complementary skills often function better than teams with similar types.

Experience Bias

One may only see the world through a particular pair of eyes. We experience life through this personal lens or filter, which is created in part by our previous experiences. From this process comes experience bias, which is another form of bias that is difficult to reduce.

Thus, a manager's decisions will sometimes be at least a partial product of his or her experiences, even if those experiences are relatively narrow and not reflective of the world at large.

How can experience bias be mitigated? By seeking out other perspectives.

Let's say you are scheduled to make a presentation. It may be useful beforehand to seek out feedback from someone who seems to have a different worldview or approach to things than yours, someone whose opinions seem to be on a different wavelength. By soliciting this different or even diametrically opposed view, you can mitigate your experience bias.

Springboard to Self-Reflection

Moreover, this type of feedback solicitation can also help you self-manage, in that you become aware of your automatic emotional responses. For example, one of your colleagues might point out that you are sometimes quick to forcefully react when challenged, in a way that might be considered overreacting.

This can be the starting point for honest self-reflection, which is essential for effective self-management. This process can be challenging – to reflect on your reaction, take a step back and consider: What happened there? Why did that set me off? Is there a pattern?

Such reflection can lead to self-discoveries and breakthroughs, which can in turn lead to valuable behavioral changes such as an effort to override hair-trigger responses when necessary. Some management experts recommend deploying "the executive pause" in certain situations. For example, through self-reflection you may discover that you have a tendency to immediately fire back an angry reply when you receive an email you did not like.

If that is the case, it may be a good self-management practice to make the effort to wait awhile, perhaps even 24 hours (if an immediate reply is not necessary), so you can consider a more measured response. The extra time to think may allow for a broadening of your perspective, so that you can better understand the context and the possible motivation behind the message.

If all this seems daunting – good. It's a sign of growth, which sometimes requires making yourself uncomfortable. But in the end, the core of self-management – modifying your behavior to get desired results – is a skill that can be cultivated. The essence of leadership is having a vision and motivating and inspiring people to do things better, and self-management can be a crucial step to becoming a more consistent and effective leader for others. To manage other people, you must manage yourself first.

5

GREATER THAN GREAT: COMPELLING COACHING TO STRENGTHS

What differentiates coaching from managing? Managing often involves day-to-day tasks like conducting meetings, assigning tasks, making department-wide decisions, and dealing with staff conflicts.

Coaching, on the other hand, is "a two-way communication process between different members of the organization aimed at influencing and developing the employees' skills, motivation, attitude, judgment, ability to perform, and willingness to contribute to an organization's goals," as defined by expert Carissa Newton, co-author of *Coaching for Results* and a leadership expert at the Center for Management and Organizational Effectiveness (CMOE).

Good coaching can enhance performance, improve productivity, increase employee engagement and retention, and strengthen the culture of trust in the workplace.

Listen and Lead

The aforementioned coaching definition's opening phrase, "a two-way communication process," signifies one of the key aspects of coaching.

As the coach, you should not be the self-styled smartest guy in the room, with your communications feeling dictatorial, always directing in "this is how it's done" mode, with no room for questions.

Instead, as a coach, you should maintain a two-way communication, even in situations where your experience level is higher than anyone on the team. Coaches are open to other opinions; they have both the ability to communicate their own ideas and the ability to deeply listen to the ideas of others.

One of the best discussions of this comes in Michael Bungay Stanier's excellent book *The Coaching Habit*. Stanier sums up his book with a haiku:

> Tell less and ask more.
> Your advice is not as good
> As you think it is.

Given this, Stanier argues that coaches offer the most benefit by asking essential questions. He asserts that the best coaching question in the world consists of three words: *And what else?* Asking that question creates wisdom, insight, self-awareness, and possibilities, he writes.

Stanier's other essential coaching questions are: What's on your mind? What's the real challenge here for you? What do you want? How can I help? If you are saying yes to this, what are you saying no to? What was most useful to you?

Coaching questions like these can facilitate two-way communication, which in turn helps enfranchise team members and can significantly boost engagement and retention. It helps team members feel that they have a say in the direction of the team and how that relates to the overall direction of the company. It helps team members realize that they make a difference.

And team members also want to know what is expected of them. They want an opportunity to do their best work. Coaching facilitates this; it allows for productive two-way discussions about expectations, results, and suggestions on how to enhance performance. Hearing that performance could be improved is not always easy, but almost all team members want to improve and be better.

The Sovereignty of the Individual

Each team member is a unique individual. That means that learning styles, productivity levels, workload tolerance, and preferred means of recognition differ from staffer to staffer.

Sometimes the differences are slight; sometimes they are staggering. But one-size-fits-all management is not the most effective way to help employees fulfill their individual potential or maximize their contributions to the organization.

Each person learns differently and thrives under different management styles. It's your job as a coach to understand these differences and embrace them. Here are examples of some things you may learn.

Let's say you are coaching a young and idealistic team member who is energetic and enthusiastic and never says no to any assignment. Assuming that the team member thrives in business, you may give him or her some extra assignments.

But with honest two-way coaching conversations, you may realize that the team member is actually struggling internally with burnout. You can then coach the staffer about work–life balance, to help ensure that they can make workload adjustments and help them find methods to replenish themselves.

Two-way coaching conversations can also lead to discoveries about hidden talents and motivations. Sometimes a team member whose current role is centered around technology may be most inspired by working with people. This may spur many useful coaching conversations, such as discussing the possibility of more customer-facing duties, or even help with a long-term career plan that could lead to a different role. Of course, it is important to do this in a comfortable manner, and not with abrupt "wow, you are in the wrong role" statements.

Learning about individual employees is especially important when it comes to another crucial aspect of coaching: recognition of a staffer's accomplishments. Part of your role as a manager is to point out growth and small wins of team members. Even a "well done" email or text message can be helpful.

Here again, the individual needs of staffers matter; different employees have different levels of recognition requirements. Some team members prefer one-on-one acknowledgment of accomplishments, while some like more public recognition. In terms of rewards, some prefer material assets like gift certificates, raises, or bonuses, while others like work–life balance enhancements like extra time off or vacation time.

Team members are motivated by different things – money, public recognition, promotions, or private praise. As a manager, you can think about reactions from the team and from other peer managers. Here, size matters; bigger organizations have processes for promotions, so it's best to work with HR.

In addition, a particularly potent form of recognition in coaching is one that cites the details of the accomplishment – details that might have been missed by others but which are noticed by you, the appreciative manager. Noticing details sends a powerful message, and it is important if you want people to think they can learn from you. Moreover, coaching that recognizes details, which serves as a learning tool for employees, helps to build trust within the organization.

Add Coaching to the Routine

As a manager, there are ways that you can increase the likelihood that you will build trust through coaching. One way to do this is to strive for proactive rather than reactive coaching. To be proactive, make coaching part of your routine, and be ready to take advantage of small issues and developments as coaching opportunities aimed at elevating performance. This will also help ensure that coaching is only limited to a reactive series of corrective conversations when things go wrong.

A good example of this is coaching on the fly in a workplace that tends to be a fast-moving environment. In this type of organization, it is often wise for managers to be prepared to conduct quick bits of short developmental conversations that have value for both participants. Although these conversations are short, they can still benefit from preparation on the manager's part, such as thinking about which work situations may be conducive to them.

Second, there will be times when your coaching needs to be corrective, but there are ways to do this without discouraging your team member. It is usually key to do this in private. Shaming a staffer in a group can inculcate fear and mistrust, and sometimes this can spiral, with team members taking their cues from you and throwing each other under the bus.

Also, be especially careful when you are compelled to correctively coach when you are feeling the pressure of a high-stress situation. In such moments, the chances of saying the wrong thing increase. These situations sometimes call for the "executive pause" – deep breaths and a few minutes to regain perspective.

Once fully composed, it often helps to adopt a measured mindset so that heated moments can be avoided. To do this, you may want to dispassionately diagnose the root cause of the mistake. Was the mistake purely an issue of employee judgment? Or are there underlying policies and operating procedures that are creating vulnerabilities? Or is it a case of an overworked staffer who is making more mistakes due to fatigue? Here the coaching attitude is: how can I help the team member do something better?

In general, this type of mindful coaching, which focuses not on the mistake but on stronger future results, shows that the manager cares about the staffer. It also helps build trust, because coaching is an investment of time and effort, and it demonstrates that you care enough to invest in their development and success.

A Coaching Culture

As a leader, you do not have a monopoly on coaching. But you can help sustain a coaching culture, where everyone in an organization is both coachable and a potential coach, whether they are a new employee or a manager, a line worker or a senior executive, young or old, experienced or new.

Take, for example, coaching across teams. In many organizations, cross-functional teams are becoming more popular as a means of breaking down silos and soliciting a wide range of ideas and viewpoints.

This gives team members and team leaders the opportunity to coach other members and leaders, even if the coaches have no formal leadership authority over the coworkers they are coaching.

However, in cases where there is no formal leadership authority, it often helps if the coach acknowledges this. One way to do this is to be somewhat provisional in approaching the conversation. Instead of saying something like "you did this wrong, please fix it," the team member may offer an observation such as "from my perspective, here's what I am seeing, and here's what the potential risk is." This is less accusatory.

Soliciting perspective, feedback, and insight from team members is also a good way to sustain a culture of coaching. One or more of your staffers may have valuable suggestions when it comes to improving your use of technology. Older team members with deep bases of experience may have interesting perspectives when it comes to historical context – sometimes, proposals that are billed as new have actually been tried before in different circumstances.

Coaching to Strengths

In a healthy coaching culture, the ongoing coaching dialogue between managers and staffers is sustained and runs both ways.

There is also a coaching trend that is being driven from below – coaching to strengths. Traditionally, there has been a natural tendency among some managers to focus on an employee's weaknesses, in hopes of eliminating them by keeping "on them." "We try to fix people's DNA, either at home or at work. And that never works," management expert Tony Marzulli of ADP has said.

But many experts say that many newer workers, such as the 20- and early 30-somethings who are members of the millennial generation, want and expect a coach/manager who focuses on strengths-based development instead of being fixated on their weaknesses.

In fact, research shows that when employees are given meaningful work that leverages their strengths, superior performance often results. Many organizations are following this finding; Marzulli said ADP, for example, has adopted the managerial philosophy of "I want to make you greater than great." The company has encouraged managers to follow an 80–20 rule: when coaching, focus on an employee's strength 80 percent of the time and assist in shoring up their weaknesses during the remaining 20 percent.

As a manager/coach, it strongly behooves you to follow your own version of the 80–20 rule, so that you are consistently coaching to strengths. In a strength-based workplace, employees often learn their roles more quickly, produce better work, and are more engaged. In recent research, Gallup found that 67 percent of employees who say that their manager focuses on their strengths are engaged, compared with only 31 percent of the employees who say that their manager focuses on their weaknesses.

Related to the importance of coaching to strengths is the added sensitivity of coaching in virtual environments. The COVID pandemic exponentially increased the number of those virtual environment, but even when the health crisis is under control, many organizations will still employ more remote teams with regular Zoom chats and video conferencing.

In such situations, you as a coach should do regular checks for understanding, such as asking team members to briefly summarize information that was just conveyed. Perhaps most important, you should be especially mindful of your tone of voice. There are more opportunities for misinterpretations when contact is not face to face.

Another quality that a growing number of staffers are looking for in a manager is empathy. Global experts say employees around the world want their managers to care about them. Team members who think their managers care about them as people are usually happier to offer their best work.

A Gallup report, *What Great Managers Do to Engage Employees*, described it as follows. "A productive workplace is one in which people feel safe…enough to experiment, to challenge, to share information, and to support one another," the study finds. "In this type of workplace, team members are prepared to give the manager and their organization the benefit of the doubt. But none of this can happen if employees do not feel cared about."

This feeling of being cared about can be sustained through regular coaching conversations, which you as manager and the staffer to learn about each other's values, goals, and passions. These conversations can be the lifeblood of your organization, and they do not have to take up hours every week. On many days, brief check-ins are fine, even by text or email. Each one contributes to the continual learning process, and they help maintain engagement. Gallup's *Great Managers* study found that employees who have regular meetings with their managers are almost three times as likely to be engaged, compared with workers who don't.

Recognize, Recognize, Recognize

These conversations are also a good opportunity for you to draw attention to employees' accomplishments. Like the real estate agent's mantra of "location, location, location," your mantra as a coach should be "Recognize, recognize, recognize."

Think of recognition as a significant driver of employee engagement. Recognition does not cost anything, and it has a lasting impact. Many managers say they often see a replication of the positive results that they have recognized. In general, there is no downside to recognition.

Moreover, it is also important to remember that, as a manager, your behavior can have a mirroring effect. Based on your behavior, team members may see how connected you are to your own work, and the organization at large. If you encourage engagement in meetings but seem cynical or uncaring in other work situations, you may be seen as inauthentic.

And the mirroring effect can work both ways. Let's say as a manager you supervise a staff of 10, and 2 of the 10 seem disengaged. Out of frustration, you may start avoiding and minimizing your conversations and interactions with them. In effect, you are following the employee's lead; from the employee's point of view, you are becoming disengaged.

Finally, as a compelling coach, it is crucial for you to establish and maintain a line of sight between the team member's work and the mission of the organization. To do this, you need to explain where the organization is going and its vision for the future; the strategy for how the organization intends to get there; and how the employee's work is a part of that.

Line of sight is critically important to engagement. Team members should not be working in a vacuum. A good coach works toward maintaining the connection between team member accomplishments and organizational accomplishments.

6

CO-CREATIONISTS: MANAGING CULTURE CHANGE

Culture is the tacit social order of an organization. It shapes attitudes and behaviors in wide-ranging and durable ways.

Cultural norms define what is encouraged, discouraged, accepted, or rejected within a group. When properly aligned with personal values, drives, and needs, culture can unleash tremendous amounts of energy toward a shared purpose and foster an organization's capacity to thrive.

Cultural characteristics often prove key in sustaining strong performance. The belief that culture and performance are linked is gaining widespread acceptance. Many business leaders say their organization's culture is crucial to business success; some even say that culture is more important than actual business strategy.

All this demonstrates how crucial it is for any organization to sustain a healthy and productive workplace culture. Yet various recent surveys have also found a widespread need for culture change. Many workers say their organization's culture is not effectively managed and needs an overhaul.

As a manager, you can improve cultural management, and lead cultural change – or even a cultural transformation, if need be. But before a culture can be changed, it must be understood.

Assessing Organizational Culture

Gaining an understanding of one's own organizational culture can be tricky. As a manager, it is likely that your own behaviors and beliefs influence the culture of your organization. You also may have an intuitive feel for your workplace and what it's like to work there, but you might find it difficult to accurately describe the culture, to articulate its characteristics, and to interpret its features.

But such an understanding can be developed through an assessment of organizational culture, which you can help lead. The type of assessment process we will examine here works by answering a series of questions that are designed to elicit information on different aspects of the organization's culture.

The actual question-and-answer format might vary, based on what you are trying to assess. A C-suite leader who wants to assess the entire organization's culture might interview a sampling of staffers in every department, to get an effective cross section of the firm. Alternatively, a manager who supervises a small department of five employees might interview all staffers.

If interviews are not possible, managers can gain a greater understanding of the culture by answering the questions for themselves, formerly or informally, as objectively as possible. One of the goals of this process is to peel back the onion of your culture and learn about its underlying values and assumptions.

Before conducting the assessment, managers or leaders should first be able to answer the larger questions: "What are you trying to create, and why?" For example, let's say your department produces or wants to produce IT security solutions. If one of the key objectives of the division is to be as innovative as possible, then perhaps your department aspires to create a collaborative and nimble culture where everyone can contribute, great ideas are shared, and people work freely with one another in productive and creative teams.

The assessment should then be approached with that cultural aspiration in mind. Questions should be aimed at finding out whether the culture supports behaviors, actions, and arrangements that facilitate collaboration, an openness to new ideas, and selfless teamwork. Questions aimed in a different direction can also be valuable. Does the culture permit, and in some ways reward, information hoarding, working in silos, and selfish accomplishments at the expense of others?

Culture Models

Conceptual models may also help in conducting the assessment process. For example, a model proposed by the leadership expert George Bradt maps out the culture in five categories, symbolized by BRAVE: Behaviors, Relationships, Attitudes, Values, and Environment. The culture assessment questions can be grouped under one of the five BRAVE categories, as shown below.

Behaviors

Behaviors are rewarded differently in different cultures. Compare, for example, two markedly different organizations – the U.S. Navy and a Silicon Valley open-source coding company. On a Navy ship, one bad mistake can sink the entire operation, so behaviors that are reinforced are rigid command-and-control actions: strong rank stratification, clear directives, orders followed to the letter.

In contrast, at an organization such as an open-source coding IT company, a staffer may simply disregard a suggestion by the CEO and face no negative consequences for such behavior if the staffer thinks that acting on the suggestion would conflict with the company's ultimate mission to protect the Internet.

Behavior assessment questions can reveal gaps between the current culture and the culture the organization aspires to. A company may aspire to a collaborative culture but lack a compensation system that rewards successful teamwork and behaviors. Similarly, an assessment may reveal that behavior that company leaders profess not to want might still be rewarded anyway.

For example, research shows that "threat rigidity" – the tendency to narrow one's focus under threat – puts excessive stress on the prefrontal cortex of the brain and impairs functions such as judgment, memory, and impulse control. Given this, a company may aspire to a culture that makes for a supportive and forgiving workplace, and yet may counterproductively reward high-performing managers who yell at others and use anger and intimidation instead of proper coaching methods.

Finally, behaviors can also have ripple effects. Facial expressions and body language are both powerful; a manager who often comes to work looking angry, even unintentionally, may cultivate a culture of anger. Studies have found that many professionals from different organizations actually feel more comfortable expressing anger than joy on the job, and so report expressing anger more often than joy.

Behavior assessment questions may include:

- Which behaviors in the workplace are reinforced and rewarded?
- Which behaviors face negative consequences?
- Are there gaps between what behaviors are asked for and which are rewarded?

Relationships

There are webs of relationships and different levels of communication in any workplace.

Loose social networks are important because they can spill over into operations, enhancing opportunities for collaboration and strengthening teamwork.

Carpools, happy hours, and golf or hiking outings can be bonding experiences, and those who share those experiences may feel like they are in sync with one another in work settings. Research on engagement conducted by the Gallup company has shown that employees who consider at least one coworker a close friend are more likely to say they are engaged at work.

On the other hand, rivalries and resentments between staffers can hurt operations. An organization may try to maintain a culture that encourages friendly competition as a means of maximizing performance, but that can mean that department heads, believing that they are all in competition for executive promotions, do not work together smoothly.

Relationship assessment questions may include:

- Who talks frequently to whom?
- Are there a lot of cross-departmental relationships? Rivalries?
- What are the behind-the-scenes social networks?

Attitudes

Some successful organizations promote a positive attitude transfer philosophy, or the concept that if management shows great care and concern for staff, and employees do the same for each other, then customer service will be top-shelf.

Other organizations do not promote this idea. In some of those places, the culture encourages positive interactions among staffers but also tolerates less positive attitudes in dealing with customers. This can make for a workplace environment in which team members bond and commiserate with one about customer issues, but the organization may have business problems looming.

Attitude assessment questions may include:

- In the office, is the atmosphere more formal or more casual?
- Is teasing and edgy joking encouraged or dissuaded?
- How are customers, suppliers, and other external stakeholders treated?

Values

An organization's values are often embedded in the stories that its staffers tell each other and tell new employees. Some stories are about heroes, while others about antiheroes. Heroes can be an ideal leader, or the colorful fun worker – employees who bolster the culture.

An antihero may be someone who has been shunned, or vanquished like a dragon, because of specific behaviors damaging to the culture. Companies with more antihero stories than hero stories may reflect a culture that has foundered without positive leadership. Stories, like traditions, are key components of culture, and much about the organization can be learned from them.

Values assessment questions may include:

- What stories or legends do people tell about the organization?
- What ceremonies are celebrated?
- What values are communicated internally and externally, explicitly and implicitly?

Environment

In this realm, there are many visual clues to culture. Office décor is often reflective of culture; photos of employees mugging or joking around at social events, and cartoon figures perched on cubicle walls, may suggest an upbeat and positive workplace.

Alternatively, posted signs with lists of rules can reflect a culture of fear. Furnishings and office structures can also offer clues. Walled off interior offices with no views of occupants inside are not indicative of an open work environment or culture.

Logos, symbols, and brand expressions are often used to re-enforce culture, and they can reflect morale. For example, to some, Google's use of colorful logos and creative design signifies its sense of innovation and its creative operations.

In contrast, an outdated or confusing logo may be a sign that a culture needs to be modified and or strengthened.

Environment questions include:

- What is the feel and vibe of the workplace when you are working there?
- Is the floor plan open and collaborative, or filled with closed-off offices?
- What do the physical brand symbols and logos connote?

Cultural Change

If an assessment reveals significant gaps between the organization's current culture and the desired culture that is aligned with the mission of the organization, then the current culture needs change.

There is no one-size-fits-all formula for doing this. Different organizations change cultures in different ways, and all have different methods and resources at their disposal. Compensation changes can be made to better reward productive behavior. Programs can be added to facilitate relationships. Training can be introduced for attitude modifications. New leadership can be brought in. The list is nearly endless.

However, although the types and modes of change can vary widely, there are best-practice principles that will apply to most organizations trying to change their culture. And one overarching principle is that managers should always attempt to co-create the new culture with staff rather than imposing it on employees from above. As management expert Brady G. Wilson, the author of *Beyond Engagement*, says: Practice partnering, not parenting.

For some, it is too easy to fall into the parenting trap. The brain may perceive shared responsibility as a risk, and so managers may feel uncomfortable that they and their employees are both being held accountable for task completion by the C-suite. Sometimes, this pushes leaders into parental-like behaviors, such as calling employees into their office for a scolding, or a scowl-filled conversation about mistakes. This can devolve into a regular practice of managing by shame, guilt, manipulation, and control. This heightens negativity in the workplace, and it can be demoralizing as it reduces an employees' sustainable energy.

But instead of parenting, the manager can shift to a partnering managerial style. Under a partnering arrangement, the manager and team members are committed to each other's success. Both share the goal of working together to create culture change.

As a manager, you can start this process through discussions with your team members, to gain an understanding of what matters most to them in their work. You can use this understanding to guide your culture change efforts, and continue to consult with staffers (i.e., partners in the new enterprise) on the development of any changes designed to improve the culture. This co-creation approach can also lead to an increase in meaningful employee engagement, as it helps team members feel that their managers listen to them, respect their ideas, and are proud of their contributions.

Implementing Change

Here is some best practice guidance when moving forward on the culture change process.

When implementing changes, think in terms of a team member's needs, energy, and emotions. Sometimes, a manager aiming to revitalize the workplace will give staffers new assignments. But too often, this results in overwork of an already hardworking staff. Staffers who pride themselves on fulfilling assignments may not complain – and they may even volunteer to take on more work – when in truth they are close to burning out. This can be a dehumanizing experience for some employees who begin to feel like they are being treated like machines, and so meaningful engagement suffers.

Instead, as a manager, think in terms of energy builders and rejuvenators for your staff. This can include strategies to take some work off their plates, such as targeted small-scale outsourcing, elimination of tasks with limited ROI, or encouraging longer vacations and time off. By being protective of team members' energy resources, you can help change a work-until-you-drop culture to a more sustainable one. Along these lines, it's often helpful to sit down with staffers and conduct a simple energy check, with questions like "What parts of your job energize you? What is it that's depleting you?"

In other situations, managers sometimes try to improve workplace culture by implementing elaborate new initiatives like recognition/reward programs, or intricate performance management systems. But if these new developments do not positively change the culture in the eyes of employees, this can create workplace cynicism and lead employees to see the changes as something of a con game. If the initiatives do not feel meaningful to team members, they may view them as another form of colonization: another imposed development which they had no say in.

To avoid this, you should focus more on what the new experience will be like for staffers, and how it could improve their lived experience at work. Aim for delivering better work experiences.

Moreover, remember this general rule: information does not change people, relationships do. Sometimes, a manager will decide that the culture is being harmed by subpar performance by team members. So, the upcoming performance evaluation is loaded with criticism and suggestions for improvement.

But this information alone is not an effective vehicle for change. More effective is a series of conversations over time where you and your team member can come up with strategic improvements together. Other members and managers can be brought into these discussions, which make for stronger relationships with better understandings of the impact of individual actions. Over time, this can lead to behavior modifications that make for positive culture change.

Individual connections to employees are crucial. Employee needs vary. Common needs are freedom to do the job properly, the feeling that their work has significance, fulfilling work relationships with colleagues, and support and encouragement from managers. But these needs are also highly differentiated. Each employee has a different idea of what they mean in practice. Sometimes a manager assumes they know what the employee needs, but later finds out they were way off.

For example, many staffers say they have a need for freedom – enough space to do their own job, without being micromanaged. But among employees who state this need, the actual amount of engagement they want with their supervisor can vary widely, so managers should not assume they want to be left alone all the time.

So, in one-on-one conversations with employees, ask questions that flesh out these individualized needs. Strive for a profound level of professional connection to team members, and to what matters to them as a partner.

That connection doesn't happen overnight; it develops and builds on itself over time, and can be time-consuming. But in the end, such connections can have a profoundly positive effect on an organization's culture. And it usually happens one conversation at a time.

7

FROM MANAGING TO MOTIVATING: PERFORMANCE EVALUATION

For years, we have heard the cry: the performance management revolution is upon us, and the traditional "one-and-done" annual review is being swept away.

Yet, many organizations seem not to have heard the news. Or they have, but have nonetheless decided to stick with the annual review status quo. This often involves managers racking their brains as they attempt to remember how each staffer performed 11 months ago so they can prepare evaluations for all of them.

Then come the formulations: a series of numerical scores for each area of job responsibility, and an overall rating that correlates with a salary increase.

If this is still a familiar exercise for you, with no signs of change on the horizon, your organization may soon be stuck in the past – if it is not already. But if your organization or department decides to change its practice, there are various options to replace backward-looking evaluations with a more forward-looking system.

Many, if not most, managers do not have unilateral control over what performance management and review systems their departments and organizations use. At the same time, trusted managers often have significant influence over the process, and also have the opportunity to work with human resources and other leaders on changing the evaluation system. Sometimes, it takes a manager to step up and be an agent of change and spearhead such progress.

If you are interested in getting involved or even just learning about the process, this chapter will help inform you on some of the available performance management options, as well as the key factors and issues and the broader management landscape that has influenced recent developments.

The Evolution Revolution

Studies show that traditional annual appraisals and the forced rankings they often employ are on the wane. *Performance Management: The Secret Ingredient*, a study conducted a few years ago by Deloitte, surveyed a large pool of companies and found that 89 percent recently changed their performance management process, or planned to change it, within 18 months.

But such a large-scale transformation cannot happen overnight. The performance management revolution is actually more of an evolution, and different organizations are evolving at different speeds and making use of different tools.

Among human resource experts, there is growing sentiment that the traditional annual review process has significant flaws, in both process and content. And the general trend line – toward a more agile system of feedback and coaching – is also being driven in part by broader management and business trends that are moving in the same direction.

Experts say that the numerical ratings used in annual reviews can lack consistency across an organization, because managers have different ideas of what constitutes a "very good" versus an "excellent" designation. In sum, some people are harder graders than others. A normalization discussion with all managers aimed at making scoring values consistent can help alleviate this problem, but many organizations do not do this.

The once-a-year timeframe is also problematic. Trying to evaluate 12 months of work in one session is difficult, and a lot can get lost in the discussion. Sometimes performance over the previous 90 days dominates the review, but that period may not be reflective of performance over the entire period.

Moreover, the evaluation of skills and accomplishments in an average annual review is often divorced from business outcomes. For example, a staffer may receive a high rating for customer service skills, but the evaluation does not connect the dots and detail the end business result, such as a growing customer base (due to great service) and a resulting increase in revenue.

In addition, the formal structure of the review itself can be inimical to relaxed, honest discussion. There is often little room for an open dialogue, thus creating an uncomfortable environment for employees. Too much formality can in turn cause employees to be less open to criticism.

And in the physical setting of the review, communication can turn out to be exceedingly one-way. Sometimes, performance evaluations feel like a sit-down grilling of employees based on what mistakes they've been making throughout the year. Many times, they don't offer enough room for the employee to comment on your performance as a manager or bring up any other general issues.

For both the manager and the staffer, the tight link between the evaluation and a potential pay increase can lead to an intense, anxiety-ridden focus on how large a raise is justified, which may overshadow the opportunity for useful feedback and make the evaluation seem threatening and disruptive. Managers may feel bad about giving an employee a negative review, while employees sometimes find themselves fretting weeks or even months in advance. In some organizations, voluntary attrition spikes in the months after the review period.

Besides these shortfalls, large-scale business trends are also driving change to the traditional review process. One of these trends is the growing emphasis on employee engagement in many organizations. Engagement is a complicated, and sometimes difficult, issue because high engagement usually depends on a multitude of components. There's no one silver bullet to high levels of engagement; factors include a good relationship with the boss, a sense that the job is important, opportunities to have one's work showcased and highlighted, an enjoyable workplace, and fair pay.

But recent research shows that the process of awarding numeric ratings in annual reviews sometimes works against these factors, as it undermines employee self-confidence, fosters disengagement, and damages an organization's culture. For example, when employees are ranked, any interactions between team members can be viewed as a competition, rather than a collaboration.

Change Options

Let's say that, as a manager, you want your department or organization to move away from the traditional heavy-handed review process and all its related weaknesses. You know that transformation will not happen overnight, and so for next year or two annual reviews will still be used by your department, but you want to help spearhead the movement to a more forward-looking system.

First, you may decide that you will avoid condensing the review into a single number. To give the review a lighter feel, it can contain strictly narrative feedback rather than numeric rankings. You can ensure that these new reviews are also tailored to the individual, who is not ranked against coworkers.

Without that single number, you may want to try other methods for determining compensation changes. One possibility is to move toward basing salary decisions on the estimated competitive value of an employee, using real-world market conditions and benchmarking data. Or you could base the decision on the employee's body of work and accomplishments, without a numerical scorecard.

Now let's say that the first step was a resounding success, and a year or so later your department is ready to move away from the once-a-year timeframe. One route is the check-in conference, an ongoing discussion between managers and employees that can be held quarterly, once a month, or at some other interval suitable for both parties.

In these discussions, managers can offer performance feedback and staffers can discuss any performance issues or insights they may have. These informal conversations can also be good venues for career-related discussion, giving team members an opportunity to solicit advice and explore career-related topics with the manager.

This may require follow-up or multipart discussions, as managers will not have the knowledge base to immediately handle all career-related queries, but the dialogue will be a productive one. It can also greatly reinforce the organization's employee retention efforts to offer opportunities to discuss professional growth opportunities and career progress on a regular basis.

Another option is a transitional strategy of implementing periodic check-in conference while keeping a smaller, non-numerical version of the annual performance review. In that case, it's likely that the annual reviews will in general proceed much smoother, as there will be fewer surprises and a greater understanding for both parties. Annual review performance topics will also likely be easier to discuss, given the regular nature of the check-ins.

The Coaching Component

As a manager, it is important for you to keep in mind that check-in conferences, especially if they are conducted relatively frequently, such as once a month, allow for more opportunities to deploy continuous coaching. Continuous coaching, as opposed to coaching that only occurs when something goes wrong, then becomes an integrated component of performance management.

A key component of this emphasis on coaching is the principle of managing to people's strengths. Traditionally, there has been a natural tendency among some managers to focus on an employee's weaknesses, in hopes of eliminating them by keeping on them. Indeed, it is almost human to try and fix people's DNA, in workplaces and other settings. This rarely works.

In contrast, research shows that when employees are given meaningful work that leverages their strengths, superior performance often results. Coaching to strengths is also effective because it recognizes existing skill sets and accomplishments, and helps team members become, in effect, greater than great.

Some organizations encourage managers to follow an 80–20 rule: when coaching, managers focus on an employee's strength 80 percent of the time, and assist in shoring up their weaknesses during the remaining 20 percent. Although this may not be a realistic ratio for you (in your particular role) to follow, it is advisable to ensure that the amount of time you spend coaching to strengths is markedly greater than the amount of time you spend discussing mistakes.

It's also advisable to consult with your organization's upper management about having career conversations with your team members, discussing such topics as how the staffer feels about his or her progress with the organization, and where they would like to be over time. Such a consultation may give you a better idea of the organization's potential future plans, and what opportunities may come available for team members.

Considering Culture

Cultural considerations are usually critical for organizations interested in moving away from traditional reviews. In trying to ascertain what kind of new system would work best for your organization, you should carefully consider what type of culture you have, in order to understand what program and tools would fit best.

One type of organization-defining characteristic is the culture's structural type. A control culture, for example, is staunchly hierarchical, even military-like. A competence culture is organized around subject matter or technical experts. A cultivation culture has an emphasis on employees achieving growth and potential. And a collaboration culture focuses on group projects and teamwork.

Understanding these structural classifications can help an organization design the performance management program that best fits its own culture. For example, an organization with a control culture may want to use more structured evaluations given by superiors, where a collaboration culture may move toward more 360-type reviews in which peers and direct reports also evaluate.

Another organizational factor to consider is maturation level. In the field of information security, for instance, some organizations are at a basic "checklist" maturation level, in which they are focused on maintaining rudimentary information security procedures. On the top end of the maturation scale are organizations at a sophisticated business risk level, in which information security is understood as a vital part of core business and the CISO is on the CEO's speed dial.

Here, understanding the level of maturation may help you understand which skills are the most vital, and thus what goals team members should shoot for and be coached on in performance management coaching.

Driving Trends

The performance management evolution is not occurring in isolation. It is partly driven by large-scale business trends, as noted above. But it is also driven by a larger trend in executive management: the transformation of managers into coaches.

If this transformation continues to unfold, "performance management" may one day become an outdated term, as managers move away from a focus on managing performance and toward a focus on motivating performance. If this shift occurs, real-time coaching, mentoring, and building on strengths will become the standard M.O. for managers, not just one component of management.

At that point, the concept of looking back and judging the previous 12 months will become a truly antiquated exercise. For the manager of the future will be looking forward – always forward.

8

DO YOU REALIZE?: MANAGING THE POWER OF EMOTIONAL INTELLIGENCE

Imagine yourself as a manager building a team. The candidates you are interviewing boast stellar résumés, and they all seem quite knowledgeable when discussing aspects of the job. Yet, you still have questions.

Their professional credentials are impressive, but do they have sufficient diplomatic skills to work well with other team members? If a crisis hits, do they have the self-control to stay calm and focused? Do they have enough empathy to avoid maintaining an always-me-first attitude?

In other words, do they have enough emotional intelligence to succeed in your organization?

Emotional intelligence, sometimes referred to as EQ, has become a commonplace phrase in many management circles, yet many admit to uncertainty of what it actually means. Given this confusion, it is worth explaining in more depth, so that you as a manager can better understand the value and application of emotional intelligence and how you can assess for it.

The EQ Evolution

As it happens, the EQ story is a relatively recent one, and it begins with house painting. In the summer of 1987, the psychologist Peter Salovey asked John Mayer, a friend and fellow psychologist, to help paint his living room.

While painting, they chatted about work; specifically, two areas of academic work they were both familiar with: research on emotions and research on intelligence. These areas were considered separate, but the two psychologists started to speculate ("Maybe it was the paint fumes," Mayer later joked in an interview with *Salon* magazine): were there points of intersection between the two areas?

They decided to write an academic article on the subject. The article argued that intelligence and emotion do sometimes intersect. For example, experiencing and managing one's emotions may involve sophisticated information processing and employ a type of formal reasoning.

And emotions can also enrich thought, the authors posited. They pointed to research that found that the experience of strong feelings can help people perceive fresh alternatives and make better choices.

Take, for example, a worker in an office cubicle who is stuck on a problem. During lunchtime, the worker takes a walk on a beautiful nature trail. The positive emotions that this beautiful environment elicits can influence the worker's thinking, so that new perspectives can be accessed.

In the end, the authors found that there are countless interactions between intelligence and emotion. The ones that make people smarter, that help people make better choices, can be referred to as emotional intelligence.

After the article was published in 1999, Daniel Goleman, a trained psychologist working as a science reporter for *The New York Times*, read it. Goleman was electrified by the idea of emotional intelligence, and with permission, he borrowed the concept and used it as a springboard for his own ideas and his first book, *Emotional Intelligence: Why It Can Matter More Than IQ*.

As Mayer has said, Goleman's ideas stray from the original model set out by the two academics. Nonetheless, Goleman's book, published in 1995, soon became an international bestseller. The term "emotional intelligence" is now recognized in Chinese, German, Portuguese, Malay, and other languages. Several major organizations have implemented EQ initiatives to increase performance.

The Importance of Being Emotionally Intelligent

Emotional intelligence, in the post-Goleman world, is the ability to discern and monitor one's own and others' emotions, and to use this information to guide one's thinking, actions, and interactions with others.

In his book, Goleman sets out the five main traits of emotional intelligence: self-awareness, empathy, self-control, social skill, and motivation. Others who have studied emotional intelligence after Goleman's book came out have expanded his list of EQ traits to include qualities like optimism and problem-solving ability.

High EQ, considered a form of social intelligence, is often a tremendous asset for team members, especially new ones. It can help them negotiate the quirks, political nuances, and dysfunctional personalities within a corporate culture. If the position is a leadership-track one, high EQ can also help those who aspire to be compelling and trusted leaders.

But determining a candidate's EQ, especially during the tight time frame of the employee selection process, is an art, not a science. A positive personality may win over an interviewer or hiring manager, but that alone is not a reliable measure of EQ.

Given this, as a manager, you should have a clear idea of the EQ qualities you are looking for to make best use of the employee selection process. Before starting the process, think about what specific emotional intelligence qualities will be best for the role you are hiring for. To help clarify your thinking on this, here are brief discussions of three EQ qualities that managers and EQ experts say are often crucial in a workplace setting: self-awareness, empathy, and self-control.

Self-Awareness

Centuries of sages have prized self-awareness as a paramount virtue. But many, including the ancient Greeks, knew it was no easy skill to master. When asked about man's most difficult task, the sage Thales replied, "To know thyself." (The easiest task, according to Thales, was "To give advice.")

Self-awareness is key because it is foundational to emotional intelligence. It is difficult to develop EQ skills or to own up to mistakes without it, experts say. In a workplace context, possessing self-awareness can mean having a working understanding of one's general behavior patterns in responding to different situations, and knowing how one's emotions can influence behavior.

As a manager, often a good way to gauge this attribute in candidates is to ask an interview question such as: "what's a work situation you once experienced that, looking back, you might handle differently now?" The responses may be revealing, as they can indicate powers of self-reflection as well as self-regulation. Some responses also indicate a recognition for the need to be more aware of emotions such as anger or fear.

These indications – abilities to self-reflect and self-regulate, and recognition of the need to be cognizant of emotions – are all promising signs of significant self-awareness. In contrast, responses that blame others or blame circumstances, and ones which reflect a failure to take responsibility, could be signs of lower emotional intelligence.

Another potential red flag in this area is excessive lack of awareness of speaking time. Sometimes, interviewers may pose an open-ended question during an interview and ask the candidate to answer the question in no more than five or ten minutes. If the candidate then speaks for 20 minutes with no signs of slowing down, he or she likely lacks self-awareness.

Empathy

A team member with empathy has the ability to be aware of, understand, and appreciate the thoughts and feelings of coworkers, and is able to see and experience the world from another person's perspective. Those with empathy are caring toward, and genuinely interested in, others.

Empathy is necessary for effective collaboration, experts say. Empathetic team members are able to listen to the needs of others, show understanding, and help members feel supported, even when team decisions don't go their way.

Such an ability virtually ensures that the staffer will work well with teams, experts say. And if the new hire will eventually have supervisory duties, empathy is especially important. Employees who feel that their managers truly care about them are motivated to perform at high levels.

As it happens, a Gallup company report, *State of the American Manager*, found that employees who very much agree with the statements "I feel I can talk with my manager about nonwork-related issues" and "I feel I can approach my manager with any type of question" are more engaged than employees who also agree with the same statements, but to a lesser extent.

Alternatively, when people talk about their "worst boss ever," they often say things like he or she "didn't care about me at all."

As a manager in an interview process with a new candidate, sometimes an open-ended interview question such as: "describe a situation where a problem arose on your team, and how you handled it" can be a good way to assess empathy. It gives the candidates an opportunity to show they pay attention to how their coworkers are thinking and feeling, experts say.

It can also be telling to observe interactions during the introduction process to assess a candidate's depth of engagement with others. Watch how they interact with others and how they respond to questions: do they seem sincere and attentive to any questions asked, or do they seem disconnected?

Self-Control

Self-control can be described as the ability to manage and control emotion by actively choosing what to say and do. In practice, it often also includes proactively managing responses to emotional triggers. Recognizing your triggers, or what pushes your buttons, is part of self-awareness, which as mentioned earlier is a foundational skill.

In workplace situations, self-control is frequently a valuable attribute. Humans may be hard-wired to defend themselves, but in tense situations, someone with high EQ is less likely to react immediately, but is able to remain calm, even when provoked. Sometimes, this will lead a person with self-control to take a second, to step back and think why the situation feels so tense.

This applies to electronic communication as well. When a team member receives an accusatory or inflammatory email, self-control allows that staffer to take an "executive pause" rather than immediately firing back an angry response.

Self-control is often an important component of managing. Sometimes, self-control can allow a manager to transform a tense situation into a teaching moment, and turn an emotional comment into a springboard for an explanation that allows for a wider perspective.

And it's become a truism in management circles that most successful executives never, or rarely, raise their voice.

Given the value of self-control, it is an important quality to try and gauge with a job candidate. To do this as a manager, consider asking an open-ended interview question such as: "Can you tell me about a particular situation in the workplace where you were verbally attacked, and how you dealt with it?"

Wide-Ranging Assessments

These kinds of targeted interview questions can be effective in trying to assess whether a candidate possesses specific EQ attributes. It's also important for managers to keep the wider view in mind, with a broad interview strategy that results in revealing discussions.

As alluded to earlier, in more recent research, problem-solving skill has emerged as a component of emotional intelligence. As a manager, during an interview, you can pose scenarios to candidates related to job-specific problem solving. Through their answers, you can assess different aspects of cognitive ability and the ability to use intelligence in the workplace to solve problems.

In general, questions about interviewees' workplace experiences are often valuable, as the responses can demonstrate how they used emotional intelligence. For example, asking about the candidate's process for dealing with relational situations can show EQ components like social skill and empathy.

An additional option is to ask a question that may solicit a story that might make the candidate somewhat uncomfortable and spur a short conversation about embarrassing moments. For example: "Can you remember an embarrassing thing you've ever done in front of a boss, or a group of fellow employees?"

Listen closely to the answer. Was the embarrassing incident caused by the candidate? Does the candidate take ownership of the incident? Or, does the candidate emphasize the incident was caused by someone else? How did he or she respond to any lingering aftereffects of the incident?

For this interview assessment strategy to succeed, all interviewers must be engaging their EQs as best they can during and after the interview. It's up to each interviewer to listen actively, engage with empathy, be aware of their own internal bias, and make the effort to understand the nuances and implications of what's being said. If you as a manager are a part of a small team of interviewers, it makes sense for you to briefly discuss the importance of this beforehand with the other interviewers.

Factors for and Against

Assessing EQ attributes of new hires is something that the U.S. Air Force (USAF), in the military sector, has done with great success.

The USAF implemented an EQ initiative after its recruiter turnover rate hit 50 percent several years ago. Under the initiative, the USAF assessed its highest-performing recruiters and found that their top EQ skills included self-awareness, assertiveness, empathy, optimism, and problem solving.

The Air Force then assessed for these qualities in the subsequent hiring of new recruiters. After a year, recruiter retention increased by

92 percent, and the U.S. Secretary of Defense called for other branches of the armed forces to adopt the same assessment procedures.

But despite EQ success stories such as these, there have also been factors working against the full realization of EQ as a factor in organizational success.

Back in the 1990s, when EQ concepts were just taking hold, the IT boom was fueling significant growth in many economies in the United States and Europe. Some of these booming companies were led by managers known for their singular focus on bottom-line profits. Some of these leaders, which often took little stock in EQ, were lionized.

Then there is the effect of education. In some educational settings, there has been increased focus on accomplishing tasks and scoring well on tests, and thus much less time for exercises and assignments that develop emotional intelligence.

And some recruiters say that younger workers that were weaned on cell phones are more likely to lack the type of conversational skills that reflect emotional intelligence, such as the ability to ask subtle questions and patience in listening.

An Emotion-Filled Future

Many analysts say that emotional intelligence in the workplace will become an increasingly valuable commodity, for a few reasons.

As artificial intelligence and other sophisticated technologies advance, human traits like empathy, social skills, and behavior modification will stand out more and more. Like culture, they will be ever more distinctive, and not replicable by machines. And in professions where technology will be doing an increasing share of the rote work, there will be more time for human interaction.

Moreover, emotional connections that are facilitated by emotional intelligence will keep teams bonded and staffers more engaged in their work. This may lead to increase in motivation and performance.

Finally, our youth equals the future, and in the case of the workplace, the newest generation is the emerging Generation Z, which includes the newest high school and college graduates, up until roughly age 26.

Organizations seeking young talent are trying to adapt to the needs of this cohort, which has the highest prevalence of mental illness compared to other age groups, according to the U.S. National Institute of Mental Health. Member of Gen Z may be among the loneliest in the workplace; in one study, 73 percent reported sometimes or always feeling alone.

More than any other, this is a generation that needs their managers to be empathetic, compassionate, and good with people – in other words, emotionally intelligent.

9

RECRUITING RECONCEIVED: MANAGING THE HIRING PROCESS

As a manager, your role in recruiting and hiring will vary according to the size and operation of your organization, and your place within it.

Managers of small departments in small organizations are often charged with leading the recruitment and hiring process, and they may also serve as the main interviewer and shepherd. In larger companies, others may serve as hiring managers and leaders of recruitment efforts.

But no matter the specific role and level of involvement, virtually all managers make key contributions to this process. Sometimes these contributions depend on if the manager is willing to go the extra mile and take an active role in areas such as recruiting and building up a talent pipeline.

This chapter covers the journey from recruiting an employee for an open position through the interview and consideration process, and offers perspective and best practice guidance for each step along the way.

Recruiting Reconceived

Think of recruiting as the artful marriage of two processes: the selection of potential employees and the promotion of an organization.

Let's take the second part first. Promotion is ongoing, continuous. It involves highlighting the organization's assets and attributes so that its allure to potential new employees stands out, which is a great boon to a company's recruiting program. This process takes effort, but it can be described as passive as it is conducted regularly, as a matter of course.

The starting point in this area is to understand how your organization is portrayed online and assess what needs to be done to enhance that presence. First stop: your organization's website.

Your website is a reflection of your culture, and your culture is key in recruitment. Having a website that reflects well on the company may seem like a commonsense truism, yet a surprisingly high number of companies fail in this respect, experts say.

Your organization's goal here should be to host a rich, impeccably functioning website, which is checked, audited, and evaluated from the perspective of the customer. Not only should it be visually attractive, but it should also be free of functional glitches, which can cause users (some of whom may be potential candidates) to bounce away. This is particularly important if prospective employees are submitting a resume or contact information through the site.

Like its website, a company's Facebook page and LinkedIn group, as well as its Twitter feed, also reflect the organization's culture. Steady activity on all maintains an ongoing message that the organization's culture is an energetic and engaged one. Posts and tweets also provide opportunities to share information about the company and illustrate its values.

Of course, all posts reflect on the organization, so questionable or tone-deaf messages should be avoided. And on-and-off efforts here can make your culture seem scattered. If you have too many sites to be managed and don't have a full team to support them, it could lead to a bevy of neglected pages that negatively affect the organization's reputation.

As a manager, you may encourage storytelling efforts by team members, such as LinkedIn profiles that comment on the company, individual posts on a department blog, and tweets about professional accomplishments. Some firms maintain a frequently updated blog where employees share stories about their professional experiences and topics they're passionate about. Facebook and Instagram posts of company events, parties, and outings also show cultural appeal.

Surveys show that a majority of job seekers read company reviews and ratings when considering a new job, so check review sites like Glassdoor and InHerSight. If appropriate, discuss with other company leaders about responding to feedback there, to let people know your input and that you will take action where it's necessary.

In public, your organization is represented whenever employees participate in community and charity events, speak at conferences, and are quoted in industry publications. Opportunities to do so can be publicized within your company. Like social media activities, employees should not be pressured to take part, but encouraged if they are so inclined.

These windows to your culture can be complemented by a talent sourcing process that periodically connects with potential future talent, even when no positions are currently open.

Talent Sourcing

According to statistical estimates, roughly half of people who apply for a job are underqualified, and roughly half of companies report that they have very few qualified applicants for the positions they are trying to fill. Talent sourcing improves your chances of attracting qualified applicants. Think of talent sourcing as recruiting efforts made before positions open up.

Sourcing can be a bridge to sections of the talent pool that are new to you. It allows you to take a more active approach to setting up your pipeline and initiate connections with desirable talent. And while only about a third of the workforce is actively looking for a new opportunity at any given time, 90 percent of the workforce is willing to talk and learn more.

Some fundamental ways that your recruiting can improve diversity in your organization include conducting outreach in local communities; wording job postings to target diverse groups; showcasing diversity in recruitment marketing and interview panels; training interviewers about unconscious bias; and involving employee resource groups in the sourcing, recruiting, and hiring process.

Recruiting for Open Positions

Organizations can expand their talent pool tenfold by recruiting through their employees' networks. Encourage your team to advertise the opening on their social networks, and see if anyone in your employees' networks would be a good fit for one of your open roles.

Digital communications tools such as artificially intelligent job outreach programs are also increasingly popular as a means of connecting with candidates. In addition, more and more firms are looking to leverage analytics tools (which can scan resumes and data that you have input to automatically surface key insights and information at a glance).

Some active recruiting efforts send outreach messages. If your organization decides to do this, here are a few tips. Use a compelling subject line on the message that will stand out and make the potential candidate want to open and read it. Personalize the message with information you found about the candidate. Paint a brief picture of the role and your organization and explain how you think they could contribute to the team.

A follow-up message can actually be more effective than the first email you send. Persistence, within reason, demonstrates interest. But do not bombard. Keep in touch with strong potential candidates who aren't ready to make a move when you first approach them.

Automated tools can help you simultaneously post job vacancies to various social media sites. Metrics can also be kept on sources of hires, as a way to monitor social recruiting return on investment.

Recent surveys show that the leading social media recruiting tool continues to be LinkedIn. But Twitter can also be a multifaceted recruiting tool; open positions can be tweeted. Hashtags can be used to help reach job seekers, but using too many hashtags, or overly broad terms like #jobs, can create more noise than value. And be careful not to bite off more than you can chew with a social media campaign, which can become more time-consuming than initially envisioned.

Spurred by the COVID pandemic, more recruiters are turning to videoconferencing technologies to screen candidates as well.

Keeping the Process Professional

After qualified candidates are located, managers should keep in mind that an organization's brand is being put to the test during interactions with candidates, experts say. The process should be professional at all times; understand that you may only get one pass at a candidate. Do your best to make effective use of his or her time. (If you are not the hiring manager, try to stay coordinated with whoever is.)

You should go into every conversation with a candidate with a desired outcome in mind. For example, during a phone conversation about the opportunity, you should have in mind what you want to propose, such as a lunch meeting at a certain time and date.

You should also clearly communicate the timeline to a candidate – expectations on when a decision will be made, and when an offer will go out. Lead the process; don't let it become a balloon floating around which nobody knows when it's going to come down.

This professionalism should extend to the end of the recruiting cycle – to all candidates, not just the one hired. In the marriage of promotion and employee selection, marketing applies to everyone – those selected and those not. A kind, handwritten note from a member of the hiring team, for example, can go a long way towards leaving a positive impression with a candidate who was not selected. Aim so that even the ones you do not hire will still want to work for you.

Soft Skills to Look For

Hard skills will get you the interview, soft skills will get you the job – and soft skills will be a key factor in determining how well you perform in the job. It's a sentiment that many recruiters seem to swear by.

And some of these recruiters (and the organizations they work for) say the most important soft skill is communication, as the foundation of every other soft skill. Communication skills, they argue, are required to execute the day-to-day requirements of leadership and managing a team. Communication skills cover speaking skills, active listening skills, presentation skills, and more.

Speaking and conversation skills are a big asset in internal meetings and working with technical staffers, as well as interacting with vendors and external business partners. In a lightning fast business environment, the ability to communicate clear and concise messages is crucial. And many communication skill sets are diversifying and becoming broader, with some including search engine optimization (SEO), mobile applications, video interviewing, and gamification.

Another key asset under the communications umbrella is the ability to be an effective storyteller. For an aspiring manager, the value of this skill begins in the interview – the ability to communicate and frame one's career progression as a purpose-driven narrative that is gaining momentum can be a big boost toward achieving success. The value of digital storytelling skill is also on the rise.

Spotting Emotional Intelligence

Besides communication skills, emotional intelligence has become an increasingly sought-after attribute for candidates in the job market, especially for positions that have current or possibly future management responsibilities.

Emotional intelligence (often abbreviated as EQ) is the ability to perceive another's emotions, reactions, and perspective, and to handle interpersonal relationships judiciously and empathetically.

Often, it is the between-the-lines quality that many organizations seek in new hires but sometimes find hard to articulate in a job description.

It has many applications. These include working well as a teammate, empathetic listening, building consensus, and an ability to be persuasive and to motivate. Humanistic professionals who have the ability to talk over problems with inexperienced team members with a sympathetic demeanor are in high demand with some organizations.

Take, for example, a common question asked in many workplaces by team members confused about tasks: "Why are we doing this?" Emotional intelligence is a huge asset for a manager who is trying to explain this in such a way that will motivate teams to embrace initiatives.

Emotional intelligence can also bolster a manager's communication skill set. Managers with high EQ are aware of their audience; they know that different team members have different learning styles and interests, and they can tailor messages and delivery to fit each staffer.

EQ is also an asset for a candidate in the interview itself because it helps them demonstrate their value. High EQ candidates are often fine-tuned to how they are perceived. They do not rest on their laurels or resume. They are more likely to actively research the organizations and offer examples of potential contributions that are directly relevant. In general, they are good at making good impressions.

Given this, it is worthwhile to be cognizant of these signs of emotional intelligence when you are interviewing candidates. Do they seem to be able to perceive your perspective and read your reactions? Do they seem to possess sympathy for others in their explanations? Do they listen well, with empathy? Do they seem self-aware?

Other Key Skills

While there is a growing consensus on the importance of communication ability and emotional intelligence for potential team members, these skills are hard to find in some candidates, recruiters say.

Some observe that overreliance on technology is eroding person-to-person communication.

This school of thought holds that our society is so focused on communicating electronically that the ability to strike up a conversation in person with another person is collectively decreasing. This is a significant problem for members of the younger generations, who have grown up on electronic communication and thus are less immersed in in-person communication.

Communication gaps are not the only common deficiency, recruiters say. In the area of emotional intelligence, self-awareness can be a subtle yet important attribute. Those who have it are more likely to seek feedback, be willing to admit mistakes, and take responsibility for their actions. Self-aware team members often realize the importance of continuous growth, and have a desire for self-development and learning new skills.

But recruiters say that a good number of candidates lack this self-awareness. One reason is that, unlike other skills that can be linked to performance metrics, self-awareness is not as easy to measure. It is also not as frequently talked about, and although it is common for young professionals to work on speaking or writing skills, few make the effort to become more self-aware.

Another subtle-yet-valuable soft skill that seems to be lacking in many job candidates these days is the ability to question assumptions, recruiters say. With technology and analytics developing at lightning speed, a successful manager can't hold on to traditional ways of solving problems. Therefore, the ability to identify a challenge without assuming that it can be solved the same way it was a year or two ago is a real attribute.

Of course, the combination of soft skills needed will also depend on the circumstances surrounding the position being filled. Usually, a new employee is hired to address an organizational challenge, and all firms and cultures are unique.

This unique quality, however, was sometimes a problem in the past, recruiters say. Some candidates were institutionalized – successful inside of their own insular organizational culture, but unable to adapt in a different environment.

Now, with businesses more interconnected, candidates are expected to be agile enough to be effective in a new organization. Moreover, some strategic organizations put a premium on fluid operations, so they look for candidates with portable skills that can work on interdependent teams that trade members or interlock while working at an increasingly rapid pace.

As a manager, the expectation often facing you in those environments is that you are able to make strategic decisions on the fly and nimbly rearrange team members as needed. You should also understand where you need to add to your team, and which needed skills can be groomed and which can be outsourced, et cetera.

Finally, when it comes to recruiting and hiring new talent, more and more organizations are finding that job skills are now just table stakes. The character of new hires – their integrity, authenticity, and their self-respect – is often the difference between adequate talent and star talent. As a manager, being open to those positive character traits while recruiting, interviewing, and hiring will be key.

10

AN INVITATION TO IMPROVE: MANAGING DIFFICULT EMPLOYEES

Problem employees. Difficult staffers. Team members in need of behavioral modification and attitude adjustment. They may be uncooperative, overly negative, excessively distracted, or simply hard to work with. They usually require a special approach.

There is no one silver bullet solution or scripted spiel that can suddenly make a difficult team member easy to work with. But there are numerous strategies, covering various parts of the process, that can be very helpful. As a manager, sometimes you may have to deal with difficult behaviors that stem from well-entrenched personal qualities, and so you need to be creative in your use of personal strategies and management tools.

Pre-qualifying

The first piece of guidance here is simple: don't let a team member reach the point where they become a problem employee. This entails a sustained effort on your part, and the effort starts during the hiring process.

A good place to begin this effort is by following this guideline: Hire not only for the right skill set, but for the right qualities and attitude.

To do this, look for indications of emotional intelligence when learning about candidates during the recruiting and interviewing process. Those indications can include relationship management skills, self-awareness, social awareness, empathy, altruism, and an amenable personality.

Once the new hire begins, continue the effort during the onboarding process. Initiate conversations with the new hire on responsibilities, expectations, and other topics that will make his or her role clear. Encourage questions to help build their understanding of the position.

Once onboarding is finished, these regular conversations should continue, perhaps a ten-minute informal chat every few weeks or so. These chats are helpful for several reasons.

They allow each party to provide feedback. If signs of unproductive behavior in the workplace are starting to crop up, they can be discussed before they have time to solidify. Moreover, the new team member can let you know how they feel about their assignments and role, and any adjustments that can be explored.

These chats also allow you, as a manager, to repeatedly emphasize how the team member's role is tied to the success of the organization, which can go a long way toward maintaining the staffer's sense of mission.

And these conversations also allow you to gauge the team member's alignment with the organization. Through active listening, you can learn about the staffer on a deeper level: their sense of mission, values, life goals, and involvement in the community. It is these types of discussions that show team members that you care about them as an individual and as a team member.

Once you gain this deeper knowledge about a team member, you can better understand how their values align with the company's mission, and the ways in which they feel most connected with the organization. This alignment of values is the best environment in which to build trust and connection. When that happens, the staffer is much more likely to be engaged and professionally fulfilled, and much less likely to become a difficult or problem employee.

Professional Objectivity

Of course, some managers, such as those newly hired or promoted, take over a department that is already staffed. In those cases, you may find yourself face-to-face with a difficult employee, with no previous opportunity to work with them at the point of hire or immediately after.

In these situations, you should strive to be as self-aware as possible when approaching any problems. Ask yourself, "Are my behaviors or actions making this problem worse?" Try to answer that question as honestly as possible.

Here are a few examples how managers may make the problem worse. Some managers may sense problems with a staffer's behavior or attitude and become frustrated, but never take concrete actions to address it, and the problem worsens.

Sometimes, a manager assumes that the team member knows there is a problem, and so the manager becomes more and more frustrated because they feel that the staffer is knowingly continuing to transgress. This could lead to a blow-up on the manager's part that is neither professional nor managerially sound.

In other cases, managers devote a tremendous amount of extra attention and time to difficult employees, and this runs the risk of rewarding bad behavior.

So, besides self-awareness, strive for maximum fairness in your approach. If you looking into a problematic situation with a team member, make sure it does not veer into witch hunt territory. Do not leap to conclusions, and to be as open to input as possible. Facts are facts, but they can change, so be as objective as possible.

Maintaining professional respect is also key. Your meetings with staffers should never have the tone of a parent–child scold session, but rather an adult-to-adult conversation between two intelligent professionals.

Overall, it is usually best to take a positive and optimistic stance during the discussion and focus on future improvement. For example, you may clearly state: "What I would like to do here is for us to find a way forward." Solicit the team member's ideas on this, as well as offering your own.

It is also a good practice to strive for agreement and feedback from your team member. If certain procedures or policies were breached, you should state those and then check for understanding.

In such cases, it is important to remember that any actions that can be interpreted as discriminatory, or as harassment, can lead to civil action by employees. Hence, proper documentation, which can show that the employee was not singled out for special treatment, is important. Seeking cooperation in documentation is often advisable; if you are documenting the meeting, you may ask the employee to agree with the documentation.

Re-engagement

In some cases, a team member's problematic behavior and attitude is a manifestation of a deeper underlying issue: lack of engagement with their job.

This possibility is often worth discussing with the staffer. Sometimes, an honest and supportive conversation will reveal a truth – the team member is simply not in the right job. That is an unpleasant thought for some, especially longtime employees who are at a loss for what they would do if they left their current job.

But if that is the case and it is acknowledged, a manager can then work with the employee on some potentially productive activities.

For example, you can help the team member frame a vision for a future career. This may give him or her the impetus to resign and find a job that they would be more aligned with. Or, they may see new value in the current position (perhaps with a few adjustments) as a stepping stone on the way to their desired career destination.

However, in many cases, a staffer's lack of engagement is not because they are an inherently poor match for the job; the deeper reasons that drove them to enter the profession are likely still valid. Somewhere along the way, the connection was lost. Often, that's because the staffer is not seeing clear evidence of why his or her work is crucial to the organization and its mission, and how that mission is important to the larger world.

This is because evidence of this importance and value can be obscured in different ways. Day-to-day repetition can make work seem rote. Overwork can compel staffers to focus, above anything else, on keeping their heads above water. Sometimes, concepts like mission and purpose are given lip service, but never explicitly expressed or explored. Once the connection is lost, it's a rare staffer that will flat-out ask management – can you show me why my work matters?

But here you can take the initiative and, through exploratory discussion, help your team member regain perspective on their contributions and value, to the organization and beyond. You can point out where the connection is, in a way that could re-inspire them.

Behavioral Specifics

Every team member is unique, distinctive. Nonetheless, there are certain types of difficult behaviors and attitudes that occur in many workplaces. Below are examples of some common difficult workplace behaviors, based on conversations with workplace issue experts as well as a review of published HR literature. Each thumbnail sketch is followed by some best-practice advice on how managers should deal with each one.

Negative Nancy. Nancy naysays projects and assignments. Shoots down the new ideas of others. Often predicts doom. Frequently makes comments such as, "We tried that before, and it never works." "This project is turning into a complete disaster." "There's just no way we can meet a deadline like that."

Sometimes, negativity is used by an employee as a badge of intelligence. Critics often seem like authorities, and so naysaying a project can be an attempt for an employee to try and highlight their expertise and their range of professional experience. The manager, then, should strive to redirect that expertise in a more positive direction.

If the pattern of negativity becomes disruptive, you may want to have a conversation about this pattern and invite Nancy to take a different tack. In doing this, use a factual approach when noting behavior patterns such as Nancy's tendency to criticize when new ideas are proposed at staff meetings. You may also explain how past failures may be the result of timing issues, not problems inherent to the idea.

Finally, you can encourage and coach Nancy on changing her focus so that the project is improved and not obliterated. For example, you can ask Nancy what success looks like to her. Have her paint a picture of success, and ask her what she would do differently to avoid the incidents of the past.

Egotistical Eddie. Eddie acts condescendingly. He dominates discussion at staff meetings. He resents being asked to do mundane but necessary tasks. His immense self-regard alienates coworkers.

While prima donna behavior can be frustrating for other staffers to deal with, a manager should be careful to keep the focus on business factors, and not on irritating personal characteristics, when discussing issues with Eddie. So, avoid saying things like: "You obviously think you're all that, and it is annoying to other team members."

Instead, focus on how Eddie's specific actions may be hurting staff productivity. For example, you might discuss how Eddie's domination of staff meeting discussions hinders others from contributing ideas – and that makes for a diminished output from the team on the whole. It is also good practice to make clear to Eddie that his team-hindering actions do not negate his own valued contributions and skills, which are an asset to the team. Emphasize that the goal is to create a positive workplace where everybody, including Eddie, can contribute and everybody feels comfortable.

Crisis Charlie. Charlie's life circumstances frequently interrupt his work life: long personal phone conversations in the office, mood swings, and oversharing about relationship issues to other employees. His life events, like his divorces, can affect performance for weeks.

Here a manager should tread very carefully. Personal crises can come in clusters – an employee may need to help care for elderly ailing parents, which can cause schedule disruptions and economic stress, which in turn can cause marital stress and possibly separation, which can cause stress for the children. It's also possible that mood swings and oversharing may reflect medical issues, which is all the more reason for a manager to be careful.

At the same time, a manager can make a huge contribution to a team member's career and well-being by being supportive in troubled times. In sensitive one-on-one conversations with the employee, you should be able to begin to gauge the level of the problem. These conversations, although delicate, can afford you an opportunity for you to gain a deeper understanding of an employee's life context – the challenges they face outside of the workplace that may affect their performance at work. It may also be an opportunity for you to highlight the organization's employee assistance program or other resources the company may have to help.

Focus on being supportive but still candid. It is appropriate to discuss how a staffer's demeanor may affect others on the staff, especially since the employee may be unaware of this, but discussions should be nonthreatening and considerate. Inform human resources about the situation as well.

Challenging Cathy. Cathy thrives on taking on authority. She will often challenge a manager's directives and be privately critical of decisions by upper management. She is frequently derisive of "company men."

In many cases, thoughtful criticism of operations can lead to greater innovation and efficiency. A manager may coach Cathy to help make her presentation and style more palatable, but still offer constructive suggestions that lead to improvements.

When doing this, try to coach Cathy to be less attacking and avoid being cutting or derisive in her questions. You can also help her reframe her questions to be more what-oriented or how-oriented, which can help people focus on the issue and be less defensive.

PART III
BE THE LEADER YOU NEED TO BE

11

New Leadership: The First 90 Days

"When leaders derail, their failures can almost always be traced to vicious cycles that developed in the first few months on the job," writes Michael Watkins in his seminal book *The First 90 Days*.

These vicious cycles commonly begin in a few ways. Some new leaders do not realize the impact of their early words and actions, and inadvertently send colleagues the wrong message. Some expend too much energy on the wrong projects. Some attempt a strategic overhaul before earning trust. Some greatly misunderstand the organization's culture.

This chapter will help you avoid these mistakes. It will also help you build a strategic plan for succeeding from Day One.

Some ask: Why 90 days, as opposed to another period? As Watkins explains, the three-month period is a quarter, the time frame used by businesses to track performance. As a unit of time, it is long enough to offer meaningful indicators of how a new manager is doing.

Moreover, in the business world at large, management is turning over at a faster and faster rate, and this widespread trend is expected to continue for the foreseeable future. This makes the task of mastering the first three months on the job even more important for new leaders. "There's a premium on getting up to speed faster," Watkins explained when I interviewed him in 2019.

Moreover, the first-90-day program applies to any type of leader, regardless if they are a new leader going into their first managerial position, an experienced leader who is taking on a new assignment or role, or a veteran leader who wants to rejuvenate his or her tenure with a fresh season of renewal. All leaders should strive to start strong so they can continue stronger. That is why this chapter is the first one in our leadership section: it can apply to all leaders.

Preparing and Assessing

Preparation is crucial for almost any new leadership role, and the preparation process should begin before the first day on the job. For leaders who are new to the company, this preparation should start before the first job interview.

If you are applying for a position with management responsibilities, begin your due diligence research on the company before you are interviewed. Then, continue your information-gathering through the interview process; prepare to ask informed questions about role expectations and workplace environment.

Some find it helpful to prepare for an interview by practicing responses to common questions. In doing so, it often helps to structure prepared answers around three fundamental points. First, my strengths are a good match for this job. Second, I am a good fit for this organization and its culture. Third, my motivations are consistent with this organization's mission. Most of your answers should fill in the various why's and how's to these questions.

This relates to another key aspect of preparation: assessing the organization's culture. Understanding the culture, and adjusting one's approach accordingly to the new challenges and opportunities it presents, is one of the keys to success in the first 90 days.

In this, staffers (either past or current) with involvement in the firm and who can speak to its culture can be helpful sources of information. These may include not only employees, but also customers, contractors, and others. Current employees can often help you learn more about the organization's unwritten norms, such as the actual hours most work, rather than the official shifts; to what degree staffers socialize outside the office; how connected and active staff is through email and texting; and more.

You can also learn about the firm's culture simply by being observant every time you visit the office for an interview. Take note of people's demeanor and interactions, and their dress. Take in the office's physical setup and structure and noise level. Do some employees decorate their workspaces? Do they seem focused and engaged? Or are there some "please-kill-me-now" looks on people's faces?

Owning Day One

Although preparing, learning, and assessing are all key components, they alone will not guarantee a successful kickoff. The first several days of the new role come with its own challenges.

First, well-prepared new leaders who are excited about their ideas should still avoid coming off as a know-it-all. Sometimes, a rush of enthusiasm can translate into spitting out ideas on every topic mentioned by others. The attitude should be to learn and listen first; all your ideas and suggestions do not need to be mentioned right from the start.

In fact, it is often wise to extend the learning process that most new managers undergo in the early days, so that it covers more than just your own department. Take a methodical approach to learning how departments work together, and how this impacts operations and culture. If appropriate, see if you can dig a bit deeper and learn some of what is below the surface of an operation, and consider what heretofore unprepared for scenarios might arise.

However, while a new leader should steer clear of presenting themselves as an "authority in everything," they generally should not show up with a passive, just-do-no-harm attitude. All eyes are on a new leader during the first few days, and people start forming opinions based on limited contact. Complete passivity can be taken as cluelessness.

Instead, arrive on the first day with an idea of how you want to position yourself strategically, and what message you want to convey. Listen and learn, but also ask questions that support this strategy and message.

For example, let's say you take over as the new leader of a department, and your due diligence reveals that while the organization is in decent financial shape, competitors are nipping at its heels. During your first few days, you listen and learn, but you may also ask other department heads, "I've looked at what you've done so far; it's very impressive. What do you think you're going to do next to stay ahead of the curve?" Such a directed question reflects an active focus-on-the-future strategy and message.

Similarly, let's say you have a new managing job for a firm that needs to be more customer-focused. You may consider requesting that you spend some of day one meeting with customers.

Here, the leadership expert George Bradt recommends following the leadership maxim "Be, Do, Say." New leaders will be judged on all three, in that order of influence. What a leader says comes third; what a leader does comes second; who a leader is comes first. So, if a new leader continues to meet with customers through the first 90 days, at some point the leader will "be" a customer-focused leader in the eyes of staff. That will be part of his or her identity.

Early Actions

Early accomplishments, even small ones, are usually a big boost toward ultimate success for new leaders. For example, consider a scenario of someone asking a team member, "How's the new manager?" It might be nice if the staffer says he or she is likable, but it's even more indicative of future success if the employee can say that the new leader already accomplished X or Y.

For example, let's say you are of taking over a management position for an organization that wants to alter its operations so that it can plan further into the future, rather than completely focusing on the current workload. You assess the operations and business model, and then identify an underlying systemic issue that is hindering future planning. This can be an early accomplishment in and of itself which will continue to pay dividends.

To continue the example, perhaps you have identified that the systemic issue is a bottleneck caused by inefficient processes, which prevents the team from having enough resources and time for advance planning. You can build on this by beginning to target inefficiencies. Moving forward, you might suggest refinements in resource allocations, which have the potential to improve work quality and possibly even reduce costs because of less outside contractors needed. Or, you may find ways to save staff hours by streamlining documentation tasks, like eliminating overly detailed reports for small expenses.

All these improvements may not be completed in 90 days, but early progress is a boost for any new leader.

Alliances and Partnerships

Forming alliances and creating alignments with other departments are great practices for a new leader. If you are leading a cybersecurity security department, for example, then alliances between yourself and managers in other departments are critical. These alliances can be made with the goal of interdepartmental collaboration, for the benefit of all.

Sometimes, the cybersecurity function is viewed as a hindrance to operations in other areas of the organization. But, if the department manager takes the time to learn as much as possible about those operations and proceed from the philosophy of being a partner with those other functions, the cybersecurity team can find ways to not only better secure the environment, but also improve upon methodologies others are using.

Toward this aim, the new cybersecurity manager can begin to educate selected managers from other departments about how cybersecurity can align with and support that department's goals and objectives. Building those partnerships and empowering other departments to feel that they have a stake in cybersecurity's outcomes – and showing how it can benefit them – dramatically improve the chances of success.

On a one-on-one level, it's often best to look for win-win alliances that function as a two-way street. When discussing issues with other leaders, two questions are often very helpful: What is a best practice that will help me in this firm? How can I help you be successful?

This is especially crucial for new leaders charged with overhauling operations. And if part of your charge as a new manager is to be a change agent, garnering support from peers in different departments of the organization can take sensitivity and perseverance.

This can take people skills, emotional intelligence, and a talent for deft explaining. These concepts may sound simple enough in theory, but the reality of major change is usually far more challenging and delicate. Go easy, even if you have mandate. Finesse, patience, and understanding the nuances of the environment generally yield the most desirable outcomes.

Building Your Ever-Changing Team

Team building for new leaders takes a certain mindset. For a new leader who previously worked solo, it requires a mind shift toward the collective.

In many cases, either of two situations apply. A new leader will take over an existing team, often with the hope that it will stay intact. Or, the new leader is tasked with building his or her own team. In either instance, one principle is equally valid: each team member should be playing to their strengths. Thus, this is a good principle for new leaders who are building their own teams and actively hiring to keep in mind.

Similarly, new leaders inheriting an intact team can honor this principle by doing a "role sort" in the first 90 days, to make sure everyone is in the right job. A good skill set/role match can mean a star in the making; a mismatch can make for all sorts of problems down the road. Experts say that one of the top regrets cited by leaders is "not moving fast enough on people" (i.e., reassigning staffers to best-fit positions) earlier in their tenure.

Two recent trends have had a big impact on team leadership. One trend is that more teams are becoming virtual, with some members in different time zones and less face-to-face communication. This trend, of course, had been accelerated by the COVID-19 pandemic. A new leader should realize this and be prepared to make the extra effort to stay in contact with members if the team they are leading is a virtual one.

The second trend is turnover. The rate of turnover for team members is even outpacing the rate of increase for management turnover. This is true in part because younger workers are more likely to leave a job if they are dissatisfied with the company. As a result, many teams are in a state of constant flux.

Again, new leaders should be prepared to be in a situation where they are leading a team which consists of parts that never completely stop moving. This may require revising onboarding procedures so that new staffers can be quickly brought up to speed as a collaborative team member.

The Future

What will the new leaders of the future have to contend with?

Culture continues to become increasingly important to the ultimate success of the organization. As a result, some experts say that in the near to medium-term future, culture will be the dominant force in an organization's success or failure.

The continuing advancement of technology and information access makes it harder for firms to maintain competitive advantages based on proprietary products and services, so culture will be the one component unique to the organization because it is so hard to duplicate. This will favor the new leaders who are adept at building and sustaining a healthy cultural environment.

In a recent interview, Watkins said he believes that recent innovations like artificial intelligence and the growth of ever more sophisticated analytical tools may have a vast impact on how work is done, which gives him some pause when he considers the future.

According to Watkins, the exact extent and ramifications of this transformation (including the impact on leadership) and its time frame cannot be predicted with certainty. But he tends to believe it's going to happen sooner rather than later. All leaders, new and not-so-new, should keep an eye on these developments moving forward. Change and innovation can happen quicker than a blink.

12
SERVANT LEADERSHIP

All types of leaders can learn from the particular style of leadership known as servant leadership.

Servant leaders are, in one sense, revolutionaries. They take the traditional power leadership model and flip it completely upside down. Under this new hierarchy, the people – or employees, in a business context – are at the very top, and the leader is at the bottom, charged with serving the employees above them.

This new hierarchy suits servant leaders well, as they possess a serve-first mindset and are focused on uplifting and empowering those who work for them. They serve instead of command, show humility instead of brandish authority, and look to enhance the development of their staff members in ways that unlock sense of purpose, creativity, and potential.

In the current corporate world, many managers remain positional leaders, deriving authority simply from the fact that they are the boss. They function in large part as overseers of a transaction: employees maintain desired performance levels, and in exchange, they receive salary and benefits. In contrast, the servant leader moves beyond the transactional aspects of management, and instead actively seeks to develop and align an employee's sense of purpose with the company mission.

The end result is that performance skyrockets, according to the many prominent servant leaders I have interviewed over the years, such as Art Barter, founder and CEO of the California-based Servant Leadership Institute, and Pat Falotico, former CEO of the Robert K. Greenleaf Center for Servant Leadership.

"Magic happens" is the way Falotico described the results of servant leadership. In other words, empowered staff perform at a high, innovative level. Team members feel more engaged and purpose-driven, which in turn increases the organization's retention and lowers turnover costs. Well-trained and trusted staffers continue to develop as future leaders, thus helping to ensure the long-term viability of the organization.

Given that all leaders can learn from servant leaders, this chapter is the first of our "genres of leadership" chapters. (It is the second chapter in the overall section because the first slot was reserved for our "First 90 Days" chapter.) Much like the previous management section chapter on emotional intelligence, this chapter takes a brief at the history and origins of servant leadership, since a working knowledge of the concept can be helpful to a practicing leader.

Mainly, this chapter explores the art and practice of servant leadership – its philosophy and goals, as well as best practice guidance for leaders who aspire to become great servant leaders. It incorporates insights offered by experts and practitioners in recent interviews, as well as findings from some incisive written work in the leadership field.

Origins and Early Applications

To some, servant leadership seems to be a buzzword phrase that has been growing in popularity in business circles in recent years. But actuality, the concept has deep and ancient roots. Moreover, it is something of a universal idea, with origins in both Eastern and Western cultures.

In the East, the concept goes back to at least the 6th century B.C., when the Chinese philosopher Lao Tzu, founder of Taoism, described a leader thusly: "When his work is done, his aim fulfilled, they will say: 'We did it ourselves.'" In the West, philosophers and writers such as Plato, Sophocles, and Cicero all touted the virtues of servant leadership.

In the 19th and 20th centuries, some of the popular servant leaders were human rights liberators. Women's suffragette rights icon Elizabeth Cady Stanton had a leadership style of supporting and empowering other women and helping them become leaders. In Asia, the great Indian leader Mohandas Gandhi famously said "Service of the poor has been my heart's desire," and he tirelessly advocated for better conditions for his followers. And in his civil rights crusades, Martin Luther King Jr. said in a speech that "Life's most persistent and urgent question is, 'What are you doing for others?'"

In modern-day leadership circles, the concept gained much currency with Robert Greenleaf's 1971 essay, *The Servant as Leader*. Greenleaf then went on to found the Greenleaf Center for Servant Leadership. Management expert Ken Blanchard became another leading advocate for this leadership style with his 2003 book, *The Servant Leader*.

The aforementioned Barter came to servant leadership by a circuitous path: working for companies that did not follow its practices. As he tells it, Barter spent roughly 25 years working at public companies that believed in the command-and-control power model and that leadership "was all about what you could do for me in this quarter." In 2004, Barter became the servant leader CEO of his own company, with dramatic success: The company's revenue grew from $10 to $200 million in six years.

Best Practices Stemming from a Desire to Serve

How can you become a servant leader? Most experts agree on a bedrock principle: successful servant leadership starts with a leader's desire to serve his or her staff, which in turn serves and benefits the organization at large.

This desire to serve usually comes in tandem with a mindset that is not driven by selfish motivations such as personal advantage. That is not to equate this mindset with that of a saint; it does not have to be free of self-focused human qualities like ambition. But it conceives the success of the enterprise at hand as not being about self-success, but the success of others.

This serve-first mindset can be put into practice from the beginning, during the onboarding phase of new employees.

With most onboardings, there are the usual introductions, getting-acquainted conversations, and explanations about how operations work. But during this time, you as a servant leader should solicit your new hire's observations, impressions, and opinions.

This conveys the crucial message, from the onset, that the new employee's ideas are valued. It is especially important to do this during the early stages of employment, when the team member might be overwhelmed by the information firehose and the prospect of integrating and aligning with a range of new operations. It reinforces the concept that the new team member is bringing new energy and ideas to the table and is not expected to be simply a cog that will be slipped into operations.

From that point, you as a servant leader should keep a focus on developing the staffer's talents. Servant leaders are always developing the leaders of the future. Some experts even go so far as to advise that at least 25 percent of a servant leader's time should be devoted to tasks that help develop future leaders.

There are several ways to enhance this talent development process. One key method is leveraging the employees' strengths. Often, a team member's highest performance will be conducting assignments they are most passionate about, yet many leaders don't take the time to ask the member about their professional passions – what really excites them and what they most enjoy doing on a day-to-day basis.

Another way to enhance the development process is to selectively relinquish power, so that your team members can lead certain projects and take ownership of initiatives, which builds confidence and skill levels.

This is a key requirement for effective servant leadership, but it can be tricky for those that equate leadership with control and often feel they should be responsible for everything. But therein lies a paradox – servant leaders that are able to let go often find that they are actually in more control, because they have harnessed the resources and talents of their staff, which collectively can guide operations more effectively than one person can.

This brings us to another useful mindset for successful servant leaders: You are not the star. You are the star-maker.

Question Close, Listen Closer

If serving the team and all its members is the bedrock principle of servant leadership, there are two core best practices that go a long way toward achieving that goal: close listening and searching questions.

Darryl Spivey, an expert with the Center for Creative Leadership (CCL) who coaches executives on servant leadership, has said that asking the right questions is the "secret sauce" of great coaching and is crucial for servant leaders.

So as a servant leader, you build relationships with staff primarily by listening closely and by asking many questions. These questions are usually wide-ranging; they can be on anything from the team member's background and professional goals to detailed queries about the staffer's assessment of the firm's business environment. If an employee is struggling, you should ask questions about what might be impeding his or her progress.

Even questions about smaller aspects of operations, such as the best use of time during meetings, can be helpful. It sends the message that the staffer's opinion matters and that the leader wants their feedback.

The emphasis on questions works both ways. You should try to ensure that team members feel comfortable asking questions, and they do not worry that you will feel badgered, threatened, or implicitly criticized. You can do this by making every exchange as calm and comfortable as possible, not rushing the questioner or making distancing gestures like looking at your watch. Questions that lead to discussions in a comfortable environment help drive the development and growth of the employee.

Carefully asking questions is related to another crucial practice: listening to understand. This means staying largely silent while listening to the staffer and making an active effort to understand his or her point of view. Unless an interjection is required, it is best to wait until the team member is finished speaking. At that point, you can briefly summarize what the team member has just expressed, to communicate understanding.

Although this may strike some as merely common courtesy, listening to understand has become harder with the rise of technology and the decrease of attention spans, experts say. For example, a leader who keeps an iPhone on the desk, and glances at it repeatedly during conversations, is not listening to understand.

Encouragement, Humility, Trust

Of course, as a servant leader, you can do more than listen to staff – you can encourage them. Indeed, in many ways, encouragement is the hallmark expression of a servant leader, and it is a tremendously powerful, and often underused, tool.

Whatever the nature of the interaction with staff, servant leaders are consistent in showing encouragement and humility with an egalitarian attitude: They don't think of themselves as superior to any of their staffers, no matter what their respective positions are.

In practice, this means that when your team members make mistakes, you do not treat them as children who need to be scolded, nor sit down and discipline them. Instead, you engage them in respectful conversation and demonstrate trust they are capable of making the needed adjustments.

And in fact, trust is a defining characteristic and defining outcome of servant leadership. One of the most articulate advocates for this concept is Stephen M.R. Covey, the former CEO of the Covey Leadership Center and author of *The Speed of Trust*.

In Covey's view, it is important to keep in mind that servant leaders are both servants and leaders. They are driven to serve, but they also possess the other attributes of leadership, like competence and character. Competence means that you have a track record of demonstrated ability and achieved results. Character means that your results and accomplishments are always achieved with integrity and ethics.

Trust is a prerequisite for servant leadership because the leader must trust that team members are worth serving, and also must trust that the staffers and the organization at large will benefit from their service.

Moreover, the practice of servant leadership generates trust among team members, who may be inspired by your competence and character, and also convinced by your serve-first practice that you have their best interests at heart. As Covey has said, "trust is one of the means to achieve servant leadership, and it is also an end that is achieved by servant leadership."

This practice of trust-building also benefits the organization at large. It helps sustain a workplace culture of trust, which is needed for servant leadership, and servant leaders, to thrive.

The Greenleaf Best Test

In your practice of servant leadership, it may be helpful to measure whether or not those being served are better off because of your work. This can be done through informal self-examination by asking yourself questions derived from taking Robert Greenleaf's Best Test. (For a more comprehensive version of the actual test, contact the Greenleaf Center, which is based at Seton Hall University in New Jersey.).

The test covers several attributes of successful servant leadership and poses a question in each area.

- *Growth.* Do team members you serve grow professionally and personally?
- *Health.* Are those you are serving healthier (physically and otherwise)?
- *Wisdom.* Do those you serve gain greater knowledge, better judgment, and more worthwhile experience?
- *Autonomy.* Do those you serve more empowered at work, with more control over their own decisions and working lives?
- *Leader Development.* Are followers transformed into servant-leaders themselves?
- *Common Good.* As a result of your servant-leadership, is part of society better off?

13

CRISIS LEADERSHIP

When a crisis hits, it creates needs and stirs emotions. An effective leader responds to both the needs and emotions of those experiencing the crisis.

A crisis can be managed, but crisis leadership differs from crisis management in perspective and vision. Crisis management is focused on the immediate effort to respond and recover from the crisis. Crisis leadership shares this concern, but also focuses on the looks at the state of the organization (or whatever department or unit the leader is in charge of), *before*, *during*, and *after* the crisis.

"Before" means that crisis leadership starts before the crisis. This is one of the most important aspects of crisis leadership. Preparation and planning before the crisis hits are crucial.

Crisis leadership should ensure that the response is strategic. This is important because sometimes those in charge, eager to respond, go into red alert state action mode, and rush into ill-advised actions.

Crisis leaders must also take heed of how a crisis evolves. A crisis can morph into another crisis. Other times, an after-event crisis takes root.

This chapter will go through all of the components of the cycles of crisis leadership, and offer guidance on each one.

Preparation

There are many types of crises that an organization can face. However, crises can be divided into two broad categories: routine and novel. Routine crises are events caused by known, expected risks which organizations should be planning for. Examples include workplace accidents, product recalls, physical and cybersecurity breaches, weather events and natural disasters, negative media coverage, budget short-falls, and personnel incidents.

Novel crises are much more unusual. Organizations rarely have plans for them. For many organizations, the COVID pandemic was a prime example of a novel crisis.

Crisis leadership covers both these types. It includes leading prep-aration and resilience efforts for routine crises. And it also includes leaps-of-imagination brainstorming regarding novel crisis possibilities – what could go wrong, and what should be prepared.

Let's take the pandemic as a jumping-off point. Now that the COVID-19 event has been experienced, what other pandemics and health-related crises could affect your organization? For example, what about an unprecedented natural disaster, or deadly bacteria contaminations, or brain damage caused by wireless signals?

Brainstorming will likely be only one aspect of your preparation and resilience efforts. Here are some guidelines to support those efforts.

When it comes to emergency preparation exercises, push them as much as possible to maximize what you learn from them. Sometimes, response drills devolve into exercises in which complacent participants go through the motions and carry out rote procedures. Unfortunately, an exercise where nothing goes wrong is generally not successful. In general, it is better in the long run if something goes wrong during the drill, which then leads to positive procedural adjustments.

Once an exercise does identify snags, follow-through is crucial. Failing to do so can be costly. For example, a year before Hurricane Katrina ravaged the southern United States in 2005, area officials conducted a weeklong response exercise for a fictional major hurricane. The exercise demonstrated the massive scale of response capability needed for such a catastrophic storm, but there was a little follow-up after the exercise to make major capacity improvements.

There's also crisis preparation that can be done as part of routine procedures. For example, your organization's annual budgeting process may include valuations of assets that may be vulnerable to disasters, so you have a better idea of the consequences of damage and the range of potential losses.

Also, your organization may want to consider working with new predictive technologies or programs that can be used for better forecasts and risk analysis.

CAP

To help your organization take a proactive approach to crisis preparation, and have a strategy in place for early detection and effective response, consider leading an effort to implement a Crisis Action Plan (CAP) or, if your organization already has one, update one.

An oft-cited example of an effective CAP is one that the Morgan Stanley Company created after the 1993 terrorist attack on the World Trade Center (WTC) in New York. The company's offices were located in the WTC and the plan outlined building routes and procedures for building evacuations when a crisis struck. When the WTC was hit by a terrorist attack on September 11, the plan's evacuation procedures were followed and 2,693 of the organization's 2,700 employees got out alive.

Your role in creating or updating the CAP will likely depend in part upon your position in your organization. Often, a leader in an operational position (such as the chief security officer or the vice president for operations) will lead this effort. However, sometimes the responsibility of creating a CAP is assigned to another internal leader or a security consultant. Whatever your specific situation, involvement in the CAP will help you immeasurably as a crisis leader.

Many crisis action plans outline who should do what when a crisis happens. This is a good opportunity to flesh out decision-making responsibilities, and decide which leader will make what call. Remember, even strong performers in an organization may not be adept at interacting on the fly under pressure without practice. Contingency plans should assume that team members will react in different ways.

Some crisis plans also describe the indicators of developments that might alert the organization that a crisis is imminent and possible actions that could then be put into play. These proactive actions could help the organization avert a crisis situation altogether. This type of planning also allows leaders to examine the organization's key vulnerabilities and how they might be protected.

Moreover, your organization should ensure that indications of potential incoming problems detected by team members receive consideration. There should be clear reporting avenues for these indications, and all managers should be open to any reports or impressions from team members. Leadership should try to ensure that staffers do not feel that they will not be listened to if they do report what they observe; this increases the risk that the team member will simply stand by and let the crisis unfold.

As an organization leader, helping to prepare a CAP can also be a great teaching and coaching opportunity. Giving your attention to individual team members about protecting operations during a crisis makes for an effective context to share your organization's mission and values, and highlight assets that need to be protected.

Here are some points to consider when drafting up a CAP:

- Define possible crises for your organization.
- Develop risk identification procedures.
- Define potential indicators of an imminent crisis.
- Define needed immediate actions when a crisis occurs.
- Select who activates the CAP and how the activation occurs.
- Develop an internal and external communication plan with reporting and notification responsibilities.
- Discuss the organization's media policy and strategy.

- Define crisis responsibilities for key employees.
- Specify crisis response teams and members.
- Name needed equipment, access and command center specifics, and other physical operations components.
- Develop evacuation, active shooter, and safety procedures.
- Create a precrisis checklist to measure compliance and preparation.

The Role of Intelligence in Preparation

If your organization sponsors conferences, gatherings, or public events, another wrinkle should be added to your crisis planning – event intelligence preparation. Not making this effort increases the chance of disaster. One large-scale public example of this that I covered as a reporter was what came to be called the "Battle in Seattle" – the World Trade Organization Ministerial Conference of 1999.

The first two WTO Ministerial Conferences, which brings together officials and delegates from the WTO's roughly 164 member nations, were held in international supercities of Singapore and Geneva. With the 1999 conference slated to be held in the United States, the White House chose Seattle as the host city. On paper this made sense, as Washington State is a giant player in the international trade arena.

But the cosmopolitan city of Seattle had many facets. As the birthplace of the "grunge" music and fashion movement, it had a growing reputation for progressive politics and political activism. It was also a stronghold of both the labor and the environmental movements. At the time, concerns about globalization were growing in many quarters. Many local, national, and international groups planned for months to stage demonstrations and other actions. Local officials and conference organizers, however, did not conduct adequate due diligence before the event to accurately assess the scale of what they would face, and what it might mean for security.

When the conference began November 30, 1999, the streets soon teemed with demonstrators of all sorts, forcing the cancellation of the opening ceremony. The protests continued to grow. The range of groups involved were vast, from orderly demonstrations by labor unions such as the AFL-CIO and international non-government organizations, to anarchists and other violent anarchists who targeted corporations and encouraged vandalism and mayhem.

During the conference, the hotel hosting one of the main negotiating sessions was surrounded by demonstrators. This was a remarkable scene: outside the glass-walled lobby, the animated protest grew, as did the chanting. A few demonstrators pounded on the windows. Inside, U.S. senators, conference delegates, and officials from around the world, seemingly dumbfounded by the activism, mulled around anxiously. How could this have happened? said the looks on their worried faces.

As evening came, National Guard troops were called in to clear the area so that the officials could leave the hotel. The governor declared a state of emergency and imposed a curfew. With better intelligence and preparation, such reactive measures may not have been necessary.

Clarity of Method and Structured Response

Once a crisis hits, you and other leaders in your organization may confer on what actions you will take in response. Effective crisis leadership depends in part upon not getting lost in the complexity of the crisis. Some experts counsel that, to help bring clarity to the chaos and make the complexity of response more manageable, it should be divided into components.

For example, Desi Matel-Anderson, the former chief innovation advisor for the U.S. Federal Emergency Management Agency (FEMA), has advocated a three-step response method. While at FEMA, Matel-Anderson headed the first innovation team to provide real-time problem solving to the Hurricane Sandy response.

The first step in her method consists of defining exactly what the crisis is. This may seem too obvious or too academic, but it is key to developing a targeted and focused response. In many cases, leaders skip this step and go right to the response, only realizing later that the nature of the crisis was somewhat different than they thought.

This first step can be done while you and other leaders take any immediate actions that the crisis warrants, such as communication explaining the situation. This first step can also be helpful with a more complex crisis. A natural disaster crisis such as a fire, for example, may contain different disasters within it. Each one may require different responses targeting different parts of the disaster, such as fire containment, evacuation, and humanitarian relief after the blaze.

The second step is to define the who and the why. Who does the crisis effect, who needs to be served or helped, and why is the effort necessary? This step is also sometimes skipped: responders may decide on a response without being sure exactly who the target audience is, and exactly why it is necessary.

As part of this step, you and fellow crisis leaders may want to brainstorm regarding who exactly might be affected by the crisis, and what the potential outcomes might be. A crisis may impact an organization's clients, and also the group's reputation and potential future customers. In some cases, if a crisis has the potential to affect several groups of people, some groups may be more obvious than others, and the less obvious ones only come to mind after a brainstorming session.

The third step is to develop the response. This starts out as an inclusive process where all ideas are welcome. When the pool of ideas is considered, knowing exactly what the crisis is and the who and the why will help you and other leaders chose the correct response.

Agility as Crisis Evolves

While leading a crisis response, here are a few points to keep in mind. One is to always come back to the perspective of the end user. Put yourself in the shoes of those who may be hurt by the crisis. This can help you from losing the forest for the trees when you are in the middle of response operations.

Once you have defined the crisis, be open to reframing it. Embrace new information as it comes along. That new information or new developments may require tweaks or changes to the response. Be agile, not rigid, as a crisis will frequently evolve and change.

For example, something you thought was a low priority yesterday may become quite important tomorrow. With social media, a crisis that is not very public initially can become much more public quickly. Therefore, have a process so that you and other leaders assess the situation on a continual basis.

Expect the unexpected. Under heavy pressure, your team members may act differently, and relationships may be strained. A crisis can set off other difficult events, in a domino effect. In the public sector, one example of this occurred during the response to the Fort McMurry wildfires in Alberta, Canada, in 2016. The response to this massive crisis was in many ways strong, and South African firefighters were brought in to help fight the blaze.

However, those firefighters went on strike after reports that in some cases the pay was scandalously low – $15 per day for a 12-hour shift. The flap became an internationally publicized incident, and Alberta officials had to step in and help resolve it. It was a classic example of a crisis-within-a-crisis.

To help deal with that possibility of a multiple crisis situation, always remember that although you may be the primary leader for this crisis, you are part of a team; any one person (including yourself) has limitations and should not be the only one responding. External parties might also be brought in to help.

Be prepared to operate in a technologically challenging environment. The coronavirus pandemic, for instance, ended office work for many teams. Sometimes a crisis will effect an organization's IT server or Wi-Fi. Data can become compromised by cyberbreaches or hackings.

Similarly, be agile in working with actionable intelligence. In a crisis, crucial information can come from a range of sources, including staffers, customers, and reports from outsiders. But the sources should be qualified, as misinformation can seep through. It can be confusing to navigate data and intelligence in this environment. Consider the source, but remember that examining information from different perspectives can provide more well-rounded intelligence.

Often one of the more helpful psychological stances for you to maintain as a crisis leader is to act as a "holding" figure. In the field of psychology, holding is when a therapist provides a space that is a respectful, emotionally caring, and facilitating space. In crisis leadership, this means a leader who has the ability to soothe distress and can interpret what's happening by making sense of confusing situations.

This is often effective because a crisis, by its threatening nature, naturally motivates most people to action, but left to their own devices many simply flail about. A leader who is holding helps team members by offering reassurance, orienting them to situations, and assisting them in working together. Under your positive holding influence, you are empowering positive and helpful actions by team members.

Complementing this positive holding stance is to ensure you are present and visible. Be reachable and involved, not detached and aloof. Here, how you are perceived by staffers based on what they see is important. Here in the United States, one of the more public examples of this among political leaders was the visibility of New York City Mayor Rudy Guiliani after the 9/11 attacks.

Giuliani was in an office two blocks from the World Trade Center when the two planes, both hijacked by terrorists, hit the towers. When he was led outside by aides afterward, he walked two miles on city sidewalks with white ash on his suit, comforting officers and citizens and urging calm.

It became one of the indelible images of that tragic day.

Manage the Crisis Lifecycle

As mentioned earlier, a crisis leader keeps focus on the entire lifecycle of the crisis, including the preparation before the event, the event itself, and the future. The future is especially important when it comes to recovery. If the crisis involves damage to property and assets, remember that recovery should look to the future, and not just restore the past.

This is a crucial issue for disaster response by the U.S. government, which has been mired in an outdated paradigm. The approach implicit in federal disaster response law, the Stafford Disaster Relief and Emergency Assistance Act, is to restore affected sites to preloss condition. But in many cases, such as in coastal areas where advancing water table levels indicate that future floods are increasingly likely, this approach is shortsighted.

As Brad Kieserman, a former official with the Federal Emergency Management Agency (FEMA) once said, "we put it back the way it was, not the way it should be." Kieserman later became vice president of disaster operations and logistics with the American Red Cross, where he coordinated Hurricane Harvey relief efforts.

This has application for you as a crisis leader. For example, if you are leading a response effort that involves emergency funding, consider this funding as investment. How might this investment be used to strategically protect assets from future emergencies? As Kieserman has said, "Recovery is the future, not the past."

Post-Event Crisis

Besides the risk of a crisis-within-a-crisis, there's another possibility that you as a crisis leader should be aware of: a damaging post-event crisis that persists.

One disastrous public example of this that I covered as a reporter was the downing of an Iranian passenger jet, en route from Tehran to Dubai via Bandar Abbas, on July 3, 1988. The plane was mistakenly shot down by a surface-to-air missile fired by a U.S. Navy ship, the USS *Vincennes*.

All 290 people on board were killed. The flight was a popular one among Iranians who enjoyed visiting and shopping in Dubai, and most of the 290 dead were residents of Iran. In Dubai, where I was reporting from, the tragedy was greeted with sadness and outrage – more than 200 civilians are killed and no accountability? A reporter coworker of mine walked through the morgue in Bandar Abbas where relatives claimed the bodies of the victims. "Reagan should see this," one of the bereaved relatives said.

The Iranian government assumed that the attack had been purposeful. Like an open sore, the crisis festered for years. In 1996, the U.S. government paid Iran roughly $132 million for compensation. The Clinton administration expressed deep regret for what had happened, but the U.S. has never formally apologized.

This outrage still lingers among many in Iran, and it continues to hamper the relationship between the two countries. In January 2020, U.S. President Donald Trump posted on Twitter a threat to target 52 Iranian sites if Iran attacked American citizens or assets. Iranian President Hassan Rouhani responded by invoking the death toll of the 1988 incident in an angry tweet with the hashtag #IR655: "Those who refer to the number 52 should also remember the number 290. Never threaten the Iranian nation."

The post-event crisis lives on.

14
Two-Way Leadership

Command-and-control leadership is dead. Many versions of that sentence have been spoken and written in recent years. Now, this view has reached critical mass.

Command-and-control leadership took hold in many places in the 1950s, driven in part by returning World War II veterans who stepped into business leadership roles. For years, many organizations adhered to this rigid style of hierarchical leadership. Leaders gave orders, enforced inflexible policies, and didn't welcome input from employees. Some leaders saw collaboration as a threat to their territory that needed to be thwarted.

That has changed. Employees no longer want to work in organizations where they must do as they are told, and are allowed no input on their role or the direction of the company.

Enter two-way leadership.

Two-way leadership recognizes the importance of listening to, learning about, and assimilating ideas from all members of the organization. Leaders demonstrate that the views and perspectives of staffers are valued and sought after, and this helps team members feel enfranchised and empowered.

This style of leadership allows the organization to make best use of some of its most valuable resources—the ideas, opinions, and skillsets of its employees. It also leads to a greater professional understanding of the capabilities and concerns of team members, which goes a long way toward retaining talent.

This chapter is aimed at making you a better two-way leader.

Organizational Values and Generational Change

The increasing popularity of the two-way leadership style relates to larger developments in organizational values and generational patterns.

Under command-and-control leadership, an organization's top executives determined its core values, and then it was up to the employees to support or not support those values. But the increasing importance of diversity in the workplace has prompted a values revolution: values are no longer imposed on employees from above. Two-way leaders understand how this dissemination of values has changed.

This change in value dissemination has been largely driven by members of the Millennial generation, who in many countries now make up the largest generation in the workforce.

Millennials in some ways see themselves as near equals to organization leaders, even though they are not in a leadership position, workplace experts say. Many millennial employees want to have their input considered, but they also expect feedback from leadership, which makes the relationship a two-way street. And experts say early indications show that Generation Z, which is the generation following the millennials (sometimes called "Generation Y"), will be even more demanding in terms of freedom.

The value of two-way leadership is also evident when team members have a deeper experience base than their managers. Let's say you are a relatively new leader in your 30s with 12 years of work experience, and one of your team members is a seasoned 55-year-old professional with 30 years of work experience. A two-way leadership style is often the one that makes the best use of that team member's deep experience base.

Two-Way Communication and Feedback

As mentioned above, at the heart of two-way leadership is two-way communication and two-way feedback. To start, there are some adjustments you can make as a two-way leader to make the workplace a more receptive environment for these practices.

Meetings are a regular component of most workplaces. Ask team members about the times they prefer for regular meetings. You may find out that small preferences, like having weekly meetings on Tuesday rather than Monday, make a difference.

Before setting the meeting agenda, ask for input from your team. It then becomes the team's agenda, not just yours. When you are leading the meeting itself, position yourself at the table so you are the equal to team members, instead of the king or queen.

During the meeting, try not to do the vast majority of the talking. Make an effort to ask good questions, rather than assuming you know the answer. Acknowledge excellent work by the team and individual contributions. When team members are speaking, control your impatience when their problem descriptions and solutions are not articulated as quickly as you would like.

Listen patiently to the detailed perspectives that sometimes accompany them. Avoid gestures like looking at your watch when someone is speaking. Attend to what staffers say; true attentiveness signals respect for people of all ranks and roles, as well as a healthy sense of curiosity, and a degree of humility. Practice "two-eared" listening: what is being said and how is it being said? Concerning the latter, pay attention to nonverbal communication and changes in comfort levels in discussing different subjects.

Become familiar with the professional accomplishments of team members. Résumés and interviews during the hiring process may not accurately reflect working knowledge or actual skill levels of candidates. A team member may have a certain useful skill that managers are unaware of. Ask about their future professional interests and goals.

In addition, ask team members how they would like to be rewarded for their contributions. Preferences on this question often differ. Some may want salary increases or bonuses; others may value things like more time off, greater flextime, and wellness benefit reimbursements. Some may desire more personal involvement in arranging their schedules, duties, and performance reviews. A few simply may want sincere private recognition.

Since soliciting feedback is a crucial component to two-way leadership, you as a two-way leader can improve how your organization receives and processes feedback.

Talk to team members about workplace culture. Written surveys can also be a good method for this. Some areas to probe are: does it feel to team members that the organization has a defensive environment, in which leaders tend to revert to one-way communication when the organization is criticized? Does there seem to be a owners-versus-renters rift between executives and team members, with high executives reflecting ownership of the organization and staffers seeming like replaceable cogs?

Are all employees treated equally, fairly, and respectfully? Do team members have a reasonable degree of freedom and opportunity to have a say in organizational matters? Does leadership exhibit sensitivity to competing values and perspectives among staffers?

Sometimes, feedback solicited in these areas may reveal an incongruence—management's intentions and actions to sustain a strong workplace culture are not fully succeeding, based on employee perceptions of the culture. This isn't the easiest news for organizational leaders to take, but acceptance of this hard truth can lead to a positive change. And asking for suggestions in any of these areas could lead to improvements in your organization's culture.

Looking for Coachability

If you are a committed two-way leader, you know that coaching is crucial. Leaders who are effective coaches often possess certain abilities and attributes: they are usually clear and insightful explainers; they have an aptitude for building on an employee's strengths; they are adept at working with different learning styles; and they can maintain patience in the face of mistakes.

But effective coaching is a two-way process. And just as talented coaches share certain traits, team members who are highly coachable often possess a cluster of certain qualities and abilities. These attributes can be thought of as "green flags"—indicators that the employee is driven and prepared to grow and improve on their existing skill sets, to learn new skills, and to make performance adjustments when needed.

In the information security field, for example, these green flags can include demonstrated honesty, adaptability to change, intellectual curiosity and love of learning, interpersonal skills, attention to detail, problem-solving abilities, resourceful thinking, safety awareness, a reasonable level of suspiciousness, and emotional intelligence.

These green flags often serve as predictors of future success. It often behooves a two-way leader to look for these qualities in the screening and hiring process, as well as in managing staffers once they are hired.

The following example, taken from a real-world situation, illustrates this concept. It involves John, who was interviewing for a cybersecurity position.

John possessed a few green flags of coachability the owner wanted to see in the applicant for his open general manager position—adaptability, intellectual curiosity, and a penchant for further learning and improvement.

During the interview and candidate evaluation process, these qualities became evident to the leader interviewing John. For example, John discussed how he had adjusted to living in a foreign country during his earlier public-sector career. Before that, he had successfully changed career. He had completed his master's degree, which reflected an interest in further learning.

He demonstrated that he was interested in moving from a safe, structured public service job to the greater unknowns of the private sector, where he would have to think on his feet and create the structure that worked best for the company. Throughout the interview, John asked insightful questions that showed strong intellectual curiosity.

These attributes made the leader feel he was hiring what he needed most—an information security manager whom he could mentor so that the manager would develop his own coaching skills and build the right team. The leader founds indications of valuable attributes:

a strong drive to learn, grow, and improve, accompanied by high engagement with and passion for the work.

Coachability for Managers

Here's another real-world example involving Mary, an information security leader for a medium-sized corporation.

Mary learned the importance of coachability and how it complemented the two-way management style she had learned in earlier training. She decided to take on her company's two-pronged problem of hiring and retention; she set her sights on reducing the failures of bad hiring and the costs of high turnover.

She drafted up some new interview questions designed to assess coachability. One such question was: "When you start a new job, do you prefer to look for opportunities to apply what you already know from past experience, or do you try to learn something new about what you don't know? Tell me about how you learned about which way to approach a job to get the best results?"

Another question was: "Tell me about a situation in which you thought you knew how to solve a difficult problem, but, as it turned out, you didn't. What did you learn from this experience, and what did you change in your approach to problem solving?" Another follow-up question she used was: "How do you think problem-solving skills can be best developed with new employees? Is that the way you would have liked to have been taught, or do you have other ideas on this?"

Mary then helped her HR manager become adept at this type of interviewing, so the manager could use it when interviewing. She started by explaining the value of using real live work scenarios to see how the applicant would respond based on his or her past failures at work. She also told the manager of the frequent good results of asking open-ended questions versus closed ones. At that point, they did some question planning and interviewing together to demonstrate and practice how this style of interviewing would get better results.

Thus, she developed a custom-designed training program by gathering new ideas from a variety of resources and programs from professional HR organizations that were available online for free, and then carefully updating ideas from a few of her own coaching and counseling training programs.

She then provided summary information about this new training to all her supervisors, aimed at rekindling their own coachability, which would help the supervisors learn how to better identify coachable employees at the same time. The training was well received and everyone was motivated towards a common goal.

Under Mary's efforts, managers learned how to hire employees with excellent coachability potential by asking better questions and spotting tell-tale answers. Supervisors learned how to improve their coaching abilities by practicing new mediation strategies. And employees were able to improve upon the coachability potential they first brought to the job.

The Two-Way Future

Finally, being a committed the two-way leader puts you in a good position for what many experts say is likely on the horizon: an even more radical two-way future. The practice of two-way leadership is in line with the aforementioned evolution of leadership away from hierarchy and toward teams of equals.

The COVID pandemic served as an accelerating equalizer here—high executive to front-line employees all working from home, in their own spaces. The hierarchy's everyday physical reminder of large corner office vs. cubicle was replaced by an equivalent frame of the zoom screen. It helped shift the focus from a top-down distribution of information to a bottom-up exchange of ideas.

The need for sound leadership will never go away. But in many respects, the future will be less about leader and follower and more about professionals working together, empowering each other as they pursue a grand mission. The road to success will be a two-way street.

15

Sustaining Leadership: Helping Your Team Avoid Burnout

Burnout is a malady ripe for our times. In a recent first, the World Health Organization in 2019 classified burnout as an "occupational phenomenon" that results from chronic workplace stress that has not been successfully managed.

And then, like many other developments discussed in this book, the trend was accelerated by the coronavirus pandemic of 2020. Research found that occupational burnout rose sharply when the pandemic hit many countries with force in March 2020.

One of the great challenges that burnout poses is that it can strike even the most productive workers and the most consistent performers, as well as those who seem to have the greatest capacity for hard work, experts say. It's a growing hazard in our age of overload, with organizations trying to do more with less, employees buried in information, and devices that call for round-the-clock urgency.

But as a leader, you can be a sustaining force for those that follow you. Here is some guidance on how to do so.

The Continuum and Its Consequences

One of the quintessential images of the coronavirus pandemic involved isolation and its silent partner, inactivity: people stuck at home at loose ends, not living so much as simply existing, missing the social interaction and banter of the office as so many worked alone.

And yet another trend, perhaps counterintuitive, was on the rise: more and more people felt burned out. Millions of surveys compiled by the LinkedIn company found that signs of burnout accelerated notably after March 2020, when a pandemic lockdown started to take hold in many countries. And by the first half of 2020, signs of burnout increased by more than 30 percent. (The same surveys never found an increase that exceeded 5 percent in the previous two years.)

One of the reasons burnout is such a pernicious problem is that it does not have to be total for its effects to be devastating. Burnout exists on a continuum; one does not have to be completely mentally broken down and barely able to get out of bed to feel major effects. And it tends to plateau rather than peak.

So, your team members suffering mid-level burnout may still be able to power through and complete an adequate amount of work by sheer force of will, but their partially depleted state greatly hinders their performance and productivity. In short, it keeps them from realizing their full potential. This can go on for months, or even years, depending on the person's work ethic.

In higher stress fields such as information security, staffers can be especially vulnerable to burnout, given the continual pressure that goes into protecting data and assets, and the high stakes involved if a breach does occur. Experts say that constant job pressure, especially in positions where many factors are out of one's control, is one of the leading causes of burnout among employees.

The consequences of burnout are varied; in some cases, they involve serious health issues. They can range from a stomachache, anxiety, and panic attacks to depression, alcohol abuse, and coronary disease. For an organization, burnout can significantly compromise workplace quality, causing more absenteeism, turnover, accident risk, and cynicism, while lowering morale and commitment and reducing willingness among workers to help others.

Fortunately, in many cases, burnout can either be largely avoided or significantly alleviated, with deft leadership, a supportive organization, and various strategic methods. But like most maladies, it must be understood before it can be properly addressed.

Symptoms and Organizational Conditions

Under the WHO definition, burnout has three major components: first, feelings of energy depletion or exhaustion; second, increased mental distance from one's job, or feelings of negativism or cynicism related to one's job, which is sometimes called depersonalization; and third, reduced professional efficacy.

When the first aspect – exhaustion – hits, the team member may feel emotionally, physically, and cognitively depleted. This often spurs feelings of diminished powers; challenges that were formerly manageable can seem insurmountable. As one expert, Paula Davis, describes her own experience of this condition: "Every curveball seems like a crisis."

When depersonalization occurs, a team member may start to feel alienated from his or her own job, and more cynical and resentful toward the organization. Work and its mission lose meaning; feelings of going through the motions increase. Detached and numb, the staffer tries to plow ahead.

Exhaustion and depersonalization often combine to produce the third component of burnout, which is reduced personal accomplishment. The depleted staffer possesses considerably less executive function: the ability to focus, self-regulate, connect the dots between ideas, strategize, analyze, execute smoothly, and follow-through. Often, nuanced thinking and strategic anticipation are the first to go. The team member stays in reactive mode, with trying duct-tape fixes and putting out fires. The root causes of problems and issues go unaddressed.

Moreover, the state of mind that burnout can generate sometimes leads to self-blame, where the team member feels that he or she is professionally inadequate. That is unfair. The staffer should not feel that it's all their fault.

The root causes of burnout are often a product of what team members bring to the table – their work ethic, how closely they tie work to self-worth, and their level of perfectionism – mixed with how the organization itself functions, which is a crucial factor. Understanding that factor through understanding the relevant organizational conditions can help a leader maintain a culture that protects employees from burning out.

One of these relevant conditions involves what the organization chooses to reward. For many years, organizations stressed the importance of keeping employees engaged. But the definition of engagement has shifted, so that many firms now define engaged workers as those with clear dedication and commitment, who come to work early and stay late. When engagement is so defined, increased effort, such as working more hours and taking on more projects, is rewarded.

But simply increasing hours at the office does not necessarily produce high performance. Game-changing ideas are not more likely to come when team members are gritting their teeth at their desk or gathered around a boardroom table. They are perhaps more likely to come in the shower, or on a casual drive, or a peaceful weekend walk.

Thus, the more-rewards-for-more-work philosophy can function as an unintentional incentive to burn out. Piling on the hours is not a good formula for generating passion, enthusiasm, and verve.

The organization's day-to-day working conditions are also a crucial component here. Research has found that two factors can be deadly in sapping an employee's resources. One is role conflict and ambiguity, which can occur when team members are never clear on exactly what is expected of them, and on what part they should be playing in active projects.

Another is perceived unfairness, which is often related to office politics. This can include favoritism, failure to recognize contributions, being undermined, or dealing with the demands of never-satisfied supervisors. Coping with these two stressful conditions may require much emotional effort, and this seriously saps a staffer's energy. Body chemicals secreted in reaction to stress, such as cortisol and adrenaline, can help us deal with difficult situations, but the brain becomes less productive if they are present day in and day out.

Detection

As a leader, how can you help your staff deal with these challenging conditions and situations? First, knowledge of the reasons behind burnout is crucial. This will increase your chances of being able to identify factors that tend to cause burnout before team members themselves begin to show signs of it. These factors can happen even in healthy workplace environments and recognizing them puts you in the position of addressing the issues proactively.

These potential factors include a very travel-heavy schedule, such as 50 percent or more of total work time spent on the road; consistently logging workweeks of 60-plus hours; unrelenting expectations of working off-hours and on weekends; and constant deadline time pressure.

Of course, proactive detection of burnout is not always successful or even possible in some cases. Thus, you should also be looking for common signs of burnout that team members might be exhibiting. Experts advise looking for combinations of the following characteristics that are different from usual behaviors:

- A sharp drop in quantity and timeliness of output.
- A general lack of energy and enthusiasm around job functions and projects.
- Continual signs of anxiety and stress.
- An extreme sensitivity and irritability towards coworkers, management, and duties.
- Significant changes in social patterns with coworkers.

When looking for signs of burnout, it's important for you to have a solid familiarity with the team member in question, a familiarity which is a byproduct of a strong working relationship. This is why "knowing your people," or being familiar with their work behavior, is crucial for you as a sustaining leader. If you know your people well enough, you can spot when someone seems more checked out and disengaged than usual.

Operations Analysis

When it becomes clear that a team member is suffering from burnout, you as a leader have several options for treatment and alleviation.

If there is a workload issue for one of your team members, you may be able to spread out the workload with other staffers to alleviate the issue. If you do this, it's important to let team members know that this is being done to gain more scale, and to reinforce that they are doing a good job.

Indeed, crushing workloads are now common in many workplaces as many organizations are actively cost cutting while attempting to raise productivity and output. And for employees who work with data, such as security employees who use analytics, benchmarks, or some form of metrics, the information explosion is requiring more and more staff hours to keep up with the processing and analysis. As a leader, you should be cognizant of this. Even the most productive team members are not robots or computers. They will wear out if work is piled on too high.

To help avoid this, consider a strategic operations analysis. You may find that although your team is generating more output with an increasing workload, burnout and turnover risk are also increasing, as is the likelihood of costly mistakes. Is it worth the risk? Hiring additional help or outsourcing some tasks may be cheaper in the long run than the costs due to turnover and errors.

And sometimes such an operations analysis will allow you to better see how and where workloads could be reduced. An analysis that is thorough and open-minded often reveals that certain time-consuming tasks are unnecessary.

If burnout is seemingly caused by a stressful job function, such as a security position in which the team member is protecting assets of great value, you can discuss with the staffer the possibility of getting them more support and resources. This may help them feel less alone or helpless in challenging situations.

Preventive Measures

Another key strategy for a sustaining leader is to take preventive measures, such as building in more resources and resilience to operations, so team members are less likely to feel burned out and depleted. Here are some potential preventative measures for you as a leader to consider.

Do your best to maintain high-quality relationships between you and your team members, and between team members themselves. This fosters a healthy and safe environment where problems can be discussed and addressed.

Whenever possible, give your team members some decision authority. This gives them a sense of autonomy and strength when dealing with issues, and it helps them avoid feelings of powerlessness that can lead to depletion.

Try to offer coaching feedback that is frequent, accurate, timely, and specific. This helps staffers make tweaks and adjustments and lets them know they are on the right course.

Be willing to go to bat for your team members; make sure you always have their backs. Don't point fingers or complain about them to your higher-ups when mistakes are made. This is crucial in building trust.

Periodically check in with team members to see how they are feeling in terms of their own energy levels and resources. Brainstorm with team members to find ways to make everyone more resourceful. Can you think of specific skills that, once developed, will help your team members build resilience, such as stress management practices?

Indeed, soliciting solutions from staff is an excellent practice for leaders because it shows that they are partnering with employees, not parenting them. The parenting style of management assumes that the leaders have knowledge that the team member will never have. This sets up the staffer for helplessness. The partnering style cultivates the decision-making skills of team members, so they can meet their own needs.

Approach with Sensitivity

Although the burnout issue necessitates discussion, it is also important for you as a leader to remember that it can be a sensitive subject. Many professionals attach great self-worth to their productivity and performance, and do not like to concede that they are struggling. There may be a sense of judgment associated with that.

Even some professionals that truly are in a precarious state due to overwork may try to hide it. Sometimes in these instances, burnout occurs quite suddenly, without many of the behavioral warning signs.

Another reason for this lack of disclosure is that some professionals fear that admitting burnout is showing a weakness, one that could prevent them from future promotions or ultimately cost them their job.

As alluded to earlier, you as a leader can go a long way by being proactive and soliciting feedback from team members. These regular discussions, however brief, give staffers an opportunity to talk through their situation – and vent if necessary – about the impact of the workload on them personally.

In these situations, you can approach a team member with a proactive goal – how might workload and workplace environment be shaped so that the staffer is energized in the office, and still has energy left at the end of the day and on weekends for a life outside of work?

Using this framework, you and the team member can discuss what might be currently preventing this healthy energy pattern from use. Bureaucratic interference? Too much work on the plate? A toxic environment, or other workplace problems?

These types of discussions can distinguish you as a sustaining leader. Even in situations complicated by hard realities – like organizational financial challenges which mean that workload cannot be reduced and resources cannot be added – simply granting the team member a safe place to talk about the current situation, and future solutions when the financial realities change, is helpful.

16

INCLUSIVE LEADERSHIP: CHAMPIONING DIVERSITY

No leader can predict the future with dead-on accuracy, yet there are a few trends that are virtually guaranteed in the coming years. One is increasing diversity in most workplaces and organizations. There is virtually no risk that diversity will become irrelevant in the future; instead, it will become more valuable over time.

This will be true for a few reasons. One is that the development follows civil society at large, which is becoming increasingly diverse in most countries. The other is that more organizations are realizing that diversity is a strength when it comes to team performance, innovation, and workplace culture.

Starbucks is just one example of a company making this realization. In late 2020, Starbucks announced it was working toward a goal: at least 30 percent of its corporate-level workforce – i.e., from managers up to senior executives – would consist of people of color. Moreover, the company pledged to tie executive pay to the fulfillment of this inclusion initiative, by setting annual targets based on retention rates.

Such initiatives are becoming increasingly common. In this changing environment, an inclusive leader can meet these developments head-on by working to advance the positive benefits that diversity may spur in the organization.

What makes an inclusive leader? The essence of success for inclusive leaders is their ability to take a giant step outside of their own minds, which gives them access to perspectives different from their own. The access they gain can be used to help create a workplace where everyone's voice is heard, and where diversity of thought makes the organization broader and stronger.

But taking this giant step sometimes requires leaders to step up their own efforts when it comes to empathetic listening, recognizing their own biases and operational histories, and reexamining their everyday actions in a new light. Inclusive leaders understand that being vocal about diversity and inclusion is their own responsibility – not just the job of their colleagues of color.

Doing all this requires an open mindset. This chapter is focused on helping a leader keep this open mindset, by examining different perspectives raised by true-to-life examples.

Education

Even in the current era, it is possible to find oneself in an organization that is still not free of hidebound practices, and which considers diversity and inclusion simply as forms of political correctness. Educational efforts may then be in order.

If, as a leader, you encounter these types of attitudes in your organization, it can sometimes help to discuss how various studies and reports, from both academic institutions and private sector companies, have shown a range of organizational benefits from diversity.

For example, organizations that have implemented diversity and inclusion (D&I) programs usually find a correlating increase in business performance compared with organizations without these programs.

This finding is most marked in instances where the D&I strategy of the organization is aligned with the organization's overall business strategy.

Another major report found that those companies in the top quartile for ethnic and racial diversity in management were 35 percent more likely to have financial returns above their industry average. Other examples of the positive benefits of diversity include higher employee retention, an enhanced organizational reputation, and a workforce that generates a wider range of ideas and solutions.

Other research has revealed another benefit: diverse teams are often more effective than nondiverse ones, as working with people who are different from you helps overcome stale ways of thinking and sharpens performance.

Another educational effort that may help those in your organization understand the benefits of diversity and inclusion is training. Your HR managers could consider endorsing customized training opportunities for different organizational leadership levels in order to cultivate attitudes and actions that support diversity and inclusion. Effective training can help self-reflective team members further develop new perspectives.

Diverse Hiring Practices

Strong diversity and inclusion practices are similar to most beneficial practices in the workplace – they should start before day one, before the new employee is hired.

When it comes to recruiting and hiring, even well-intentioned leaders might unwittingly make assumptions based on stereotypes and bias. To identify these cognitive barriers, some leaders need to challenge themselves – or be challenged by their peers or teams – to find out why they make certain decisions.

If you are serving as a hiring manager for your department, you may consider using gender-neutral job descriptions and/or automated systems that blind out demographic characteristics in the résumé review process. In this way, hiring decisions will be based on predefined job criteria that are verified and supported by candidate attributes exclusive of their demographic characteristics.

In addition, when recruiting and interviewing, you may look at an applicant's professional and educational background for evidence of diversity strengths – such as foreign language ability or residence in another country – that will help your organization build a diverse and inclusive workforce.

As an additional step, consider using multiple interview feedback sources to solicit different perspectives and outside views. For example, it can be a good practice to establish an interview panel represented by various organizational stakeholders during the interview process, and to consider their unique perspectives when deciding on a candidate. Asking targeted questions about diversity experience during the interview process can also be helpful.

Remember that new hiring opportunities offer an inclusive leader the chance to create a diverse workforce with balanced and innovative teams, and to break away from the habit of drawing on the usual pool of similar candidates. For example, experience in project management, business operations, and other functions may provide a great foundation on which other skills and specialized knowledge can be built.

Another dimension new hires can be assessed on is cultural fit versus cultural add. For years, hiring managers have used the "Will they fit in with our company culture?" question as a key one in the hiring process. But another question can be just as vital: "Will they broaden our culture so that it becomes more attractive and welcoming to other new talent?" Cultural adds can also help drive targeted and purposeful innovation.

Othering

Of course, inclusive leaders realize that diverse hiring practices are not enough. Organizations risk employee disengagement and attrition if diverse hires do not feel included and accepted. If team members don't feel like a full-fledged part of the organization, it will be hard to retain them in the long run.

Achieving this level of true diversity and inclusion is not easy. It may take culture change, as well as ongoing maintenance to ensure that differing opinions are respected and people are encouraged to be themselves. In fact, many experts say building and sustaining diverse teams will soon become a required leadership skillset for many leaders.

To better understand the status quo of your team, it is often wise to simply ask team members how they feel about the workplace. By kicking off that conversation, you will be able to find out more about individual behavior and the team's diversity culture.

To some extent, most team members view issues through their own backgrounds and experience bases, as well as their cultural, ethnic, and generational identities. And so, issues involving shifting social and professional norms can spur differences in opinion, which may create tension. Some leaders inadvertently trigger a conflict by taking a side.

Consider this example, taken from an organization located near Washington, D.C., a city which has a storied African American cultural heritage. At this organization, the CEO made efforts to sustain a positive workplace environment and encouraged staff members to have fun during staff meetings, such as using humor and pop culture images in work-related presentations.

At one meeting, a few manager-level white team members gave the CEO, also white, a cartoon picture of himself as a rap artist, wearing much bling and captioned with an exaggerated rapper-like name. Clearly, the joke was not mean-spirited; it played on the pale-skinned CEO's cliched "very white" image and demeanor.

Think about the possible message such an incident could send to African American team members. Hip-hop has shaped popular music for decades; its cultural impact has been immense. A staff member who is a fan of the music may consider it a proud achievement of his or her culture. Might the message of the incident be that part of the staffer's culture is something of a joke, something that some leaders in the organizer's leaders make fun of?

Going deeper: can this be experienced as a way for the (generally white) leaders of the firm to assert a form of dominance over black workers, by implying that parts of their culture are somewhere laughable and inferior? At the very least, the incident may have the uncomfortable effect of "othering" some African American employees, and work against feelings of belonging.

These issues and situations are worth considering on a case-by-case basis. Sometimes, seemingly trivial situations can become last-straw incidents for team members, collapsing their sense of acceptance and motivating them into looking for new opportunities.

Discussions and Flashpoints

In a diverse and inclusive healthy workplace, different viewpoints and perspectives are welcome, and seen as a strength. But sometimes, difficult situations and dramatic events like a public events crisis can stir emotions that lead to conflict.

Here are two scenarios derived from real-life events.

An inclusive leader at a university, a department chair, has helped assembled a diverse faculty team, comprised of excellent teachers and scholars of different backgrounds, races, and religions.

On the morning of September 11, 2001, many members still go to their academic offices at the university, which was not near the two attack sites and stayed open for classes. A few faculty members, all well informed, articulate, and opinionated, start discussing the events. With emotions still raw from the attacks, the discussion turns into a heated political argument. It does not end until one member has to go teach a class.

In the second scenario, a CISO comes to work the morning after Barack Obama was elected U.S. president in November 2008. Two team members are already in a discussion about the election, racism, and politics. The two staffers have deeply held views that are almost diametrically opposed.

The disagreement spiraled into a heated argument. Because the conversation potentially affected not only the relationship of the two officers but also the safety of our operations, the CISO decided to move one officer to another part of the facility for the rest of the shift, to ensure a cool-down period.

As an inclusive leader, think about how you might approach these two scenarios and consider what you would do. One potential lesson is the need for clear HR policies that discourage employees from engaging in potentially harmful nonwork-related conversations. If no such policies exist, consider working with HR on drafting some.

These policies should not focus on banning certain topics of conversation, but on the broader goal of avoiding situations that make the workplace hostile. Those situations include harassment, bullying, and verbal attacks and statements that are racist, discriminatory, or insulting. Two team members can have a respectful conversation about a political topic and not violate policy, but should their conversation dissolve into inappropriate behavior, the inclusive leaders should step in, and the organization should have a policy in place to support shutting down violations.

Walk a Mile in Kitten Heels

The next example bears some fruitful examination. When Nóirín O'Sullivan, currently the United Nation's assistant secretary-general for safety and security, began her career with Ireland's An Garda Síochána police service back in 1981, the uniform code for female officers was a skirt paired with the short stiletto shoes known as "kitten heels."

"Trying to chase around a criminal in kitten heels doesn't go very well," she said to me with a laugh during a 2019 interview.

And up until 1979, Ireland maintained a marriage ban that forced women to leave public service upon matrimony. That helped make An Garda Síochána, the Irish police service, a nearly exclusively male organization when she joined – significantly less than 1 percent female. The few women on the force were usually consigned to administrative roles.

Still, O'Sullivan persisted: she wanted to work in operations. So, she started working in an undercover unit ("mockies," in the local parlance) with several male officers. As the years went by, she shot up the ranks.

In 2014, she became the first female commissioner of Garda, responsible for leading a worldwide force of 16,000 officers and other personnel.

While O'Sullivan's career may be more high-profile than most, you may have at least one female team member who has been in the workforce for decades and has experienced some form of discrimination, harassment, and other career hindrances due to her gender. This experience base could be a valuable resource for you as an inclusive leader; consulting this team member to get her perspective on workplace issues related to gender and age may turn out to be valuable.

In the interview referenced above, O'Sullivan advised female professionals in male-dominated professions to make a strong effort to establish credibility with male peers. This is something to keep in mind as an inclusive leader. Make it your goal that your workplace culture is such that professionals come in with equal credibility, regardless of gender.

Values at the Core of Mission

Many organizations have taken the time to document purpose, vision, and values in a detailed mission statement. When documenting these core values, it is often worth emphasizing specific aspects of the culture, such as diversity, inclusion, and wellness.

At some point, you may have an opportunity to work with other organization leaders in drafting up a mission statement. If you find your organization's current mission statement lacking in this regard, you as an inclusive leader may decide to lead an effort to review and expand the existing one. It is an effort worth considering.

If you move forward in this, remember that these statements require thoughtfulness, not simply a cut-and-paste addition of boilerplate diversity language. You and other leaders involved should ask themselves: what are the values that our policies of diversity and inclusion are based on?

For example, you and other leaders may decide that the concept of inclusion, in your department or organization, is based on the idea that all employees are heard. That each team member has a voice in policies, cultural norms, and proposed solutions to challenges and issues that arise. Inclusion may also be based on the concept that everyone's work is meaningful to the organization and makes a difference.

Moreover, this type of inclusion helps foster a culture where ideas are sought after.

This encourages innovation. In this culture, leaders and managers also strive to ensure that each team member understands how their work makes a difference.

In addition, your organization's values may include a commitment to building a disability inclusive workplace. This may lead your organization to promote equal opportunities and professional development for staffers with disabilities, such as organization-sponsored programs that help jobseekers with disabilities learn more about career opportunities available within the firm.

Communicating these values and their specific-related goals is an excellent way to flesh out a detailed mission and vision statement. It codifies diversity into a core organizational principle. As an inclusive leader, it is a move you can wholly support.

17

COMPELLING LEADERSHIP:
CONNECTING WITH
FOLLOWERS AND ALLIES

Consider a few words on leadership by one of the greatest and most imaginative American writers of the contemporary era, David Foster Wallace. The words come from an acclaimed essay on leadership and politics that Wallace wrote after covering the upstart U.S. presidential campaign of Republican Senator John McCain in 2000.

"A leader's real 'authority' is a power you voluntarily give him, and you grant him this authority not with resentment or resignation, but happily," Wallace wrote. "Deep down, you almost always like how a real leader makes you feel, the way you find yourself working harder and pushing yourself and thinking in ways you couldn't ever get to on your own."

"Deep down, you almost always like how a real leader makes you feel." The phrase echoes the words of another classic American writer, poet Maya Angelou: "I've learned that people will forget what you said, people will forget what you did, but people will never forget how you made them feel."

If you are lucky, you have met that special kind of leader. He or she could have been almost anybody: a teacher, a manager, a CEO. These special leaders may differ widely in personality and working style, but they all share one quality: people are compelled to follow them, and do so willingly.

Leadership expert Darlene Hunter once described what it was like to work for the most effective leader she's ever encountered in this way: "If this particular leader asked me to work in Alaska, I would simply ask, 'When, and where do you want me?'"

What, exactly, makes these special leaders so compelling? Their effect on those who work for them can be mysterious; some followers say it just seems to happen, without intentional effort. We may first be drawn to them on a subconscious level, and then only realize later, at some point down the road, that we have committed ourselves to that individual's leadership.

So, when a staffer encounters a leader who encourages his or her followers to stretch themselves, who maintains a supportive environment for innovation, who gives team members enough time and space to grow and achieve, and who really listens, the clear message for the employee is: I will benefit from working here. I can reach my potential with this leader.

Let's dive deep into the concept of compelling leadership, break down its common components and qualities. If you take the time, effort, and actions required to develop these attributes, you may make tremendous progress toward becoming a leader your team members feel compelled to follow – because of the way that you make your followers feel.

Emotions in Motion, for the Greater Good

In trying to better understand compelling leadership, it helps to make the distinction between managers and leaders.

Management as practiced today is often focused on bottom-line, dollars-and-cents realities, and sometimes on professional advantage. Some managers are primarily concerned with how they are assessed by upper management. These concerns may advance career success and enterprise profitability, but they are largely devoid of the human element necessary to maintain momentum.

Leadership, on the other hand, operates on another plane entirely. Leaders can think outside the box, take the long view, and see the big picture. They are in tune with the human element that drives operations forward and are adept at voluntarily getting better performance from their teams. They can effect change, inspire people, and boost morale. As a result, team members are more likely to be actively engaged in their jobs and vested in outcomes, instead of merely clocking in eight hours.

What does it mean to be "in tune with the human element?" The compelling leader's emotional range includes both strength and sensitivity, and it translates into an emotional intelligence that connects the leader with the team. They tap into emotions on particular issues and show team members the right path to address concerns.

This emotional range was once described by Nelson Mandela, the anti-apartheid revolutionary who endured 27 years in prison to become president of his country, South Africa. "Leaders must be tough enough to fight, tender enough to cry, human enough to make mistakes, humble enough to admit them, strong enough to absorb the pain, and resilient enough to bounce back and keep on moving," Mandela said.

Of course, having this range does not mean that a leader must be highly demonstrative in his or her emotions. The key concept here is the connection through emotion. When a leader's passion for a mission is clear, it naturally follows that they can lead by example, even at times when they are not consciously trying to transfer new skills to their followers.

Moreover, a compelling leader's passion for mission is a passion for the greater good. This is also a crucial connection. Immoral leaders, such as power-hungry dictators, may be compelling to some drawn to authoritarian strongmen. But those authoritarians use devious means like emotional manipulation to gain followers toward their evil ends, like absolute power.

The morally compelling leader takes their charges forward to a new destination – in a word, progress – that will be better than the current status quo. In that sense, the compelling leaders' stock in trade is hope, which is too often undervalued.

Risk

Another attribute compelling leaders have that reinforces their inspirational and charismatic qualities is a willingness to take risks.

Take, for example, leadership in the information security field. The overwhelming number of areas that need funding – including software, hardware, training, and equipment – may mean that the leader needs to take risks in deciding how to use scarce resources in a way that will protect the organization today, tomorrow, and in the future.

But generally, compelling leaders make sure that the risks they take are calculated ones. Often, compelling leaders make risk-taking look easy because they have calculated a myriad of factors, including capabilities and limitations, prior to even presenting a proposal.

Besides being risk-takers themselves, compelling leaders also pass on this attitude to their staff. In part, the leaders do this by creating a safe environment for team members to take ambitious actions – and, sometimes, to fail. They make staffers feel that making a mistake is not the end of the world, that ultimately they will be able to do whatever is expected, and more.

Indeed, a safe and supportive workplace is the best type of environment for creating sustainable change. Human behavior expert Abraham Maslow asserted that people are often more motivated to avoid failure rather than to strive for success. Fighting against this, a compelling leader asks people to step up, and provides a supportive environment for doing so.

Inspiring staff to take risks is related to another attribute of leadership: compelling leaders empower. As a compelling leader, you can do this in various ways. One is through consistent recognition of staff accomplishments, which makes team members feel great about being part of the company or organization. They feel valued and appreciated and feel that what they contribute is important.

Another way to empower is by not being interested in maintaining a hierarchical, micromanaged relationship of the "I'm the boss – and you work for me" variety. In other words, you do not demand fealty. Instead, your staffers feel like an integral part of the team and feel more like a business partner than a subordinate, even though they appreciate that you make the final decisions.

In addition, you can defer to them when possible, especially if it allows you to focus on bigger issues. This, too, allows team members to feel more vested in the process and grow professionally.

That sense of partnership also holds true when it comes to communication. Compelling leaders have great communication skills, and these skills work both ways. Compelling leaders are superb listeners. This is a rare skill, and if you develop yourself into a superb listener, it will set you apart.

Listening helps respect flow in both directions. Team members appreciate your keen interest in them, as well as your own abilities and achievements. They are more likely to feel that the mission will be enhanced – as well as their personal career development goals – by following your lead. They feel you respect their potential, abilities, and ideas.

Being Compelling to Allies

Leaders, even the most compelling ones, need allies to be successful. This is particularly true at the executive level and in the C-suite of their organizations. But some leaders face challenges in this area.

For example, take a leader like a CISO. On paper, the CISO may be ranked on the same level as other C-suite executives, as high up in the management tier as the chief operations officer, for example. Yet it may not always seem that way in practice.

Sometimes, a leader such as an information security executive may be pigeonholed as the firm's "tech cop" – serving a crucial function, certainly, but not thought of as a true business leader in the same way that the organization's other executives are. This can be particularly true if the CISO has less formal business school training than his or her executive peers, which can lead to feelings like being an "other" in the world of upper management.

But if you are one of these specialized leaders, second-tier status is not a *fait accompli* for you. With effort, you can be a leader who is compelling to fellow leaders, who builds bridges with other executives and fosters alliances.

Sometimes a good first step is to ask for one-on-one meetings with fellow leaders. You may propose an informal information exchange of sorts that may benefit both parties: each person will brief the other on your respective department's operations.

Although the meeting may be informal, it is best to prepare for it. Make sure you can demonstrate a working knowledge of the business and strategic goals of the organization. Be conscious of the financial ramifications of the operations under discussion, and the balance between the necessary costs of doing business and the relevant budget issues. A brief informal summary analysis that you can present to illustrate a concept may be effective.

Moreover, always treat these meetings as a two-way street. They are an opportunity for discussing operations and strategy, but also to listen deeply to find out what other leaders may need. You may discover that you can help them.

Indeed, many experts say that successful alliances between leaders are built primarily on effective communication. If you feel that you could sometimes use some help in the crisp and clear expression of ideas and making proposals to other leaders in meetings, consider the S.M.A.R.T. system of business communication, put forth by author Stephanie Palmer in her book *Good in a Room*.

Palmer, the former director of creative affairs at MGM Pictures, posits that to transmit ideas in a powerful way, the communication should be S.M.A.R.T.: Simple, Memorable, Accurate, Repeatable, and Tonally Correct. (Other experts use SMART to mean slightly different criteria, such as specific, measurable, achievable, relevant, and timely.) These concepts can be helpful when preparing for a meeting, so that you strive to make what you will suggest not only clear (simple, accurate) and memorable but well-encapsulated (repeatable), so that people can easily repeat and share it.

As for the last concept of "tonally correct," this can be explained by way of a movie example. Some Hollywood producers were about to release a film called *$3,000 a Night.* They hoped for a hit, but at the last minute, concerns were raised. The title, with its crass ring of upscale prostitution, seemed tone deaf, and it could turn off a sizable segment of the moviegoing public. So, executives decided to make a language change and revised the title to *Pretty Woman.* The tone of the new title was much more appropriate for the audience, and it made a huge difference in terms of success.

Another principle of effective communication that can help you as a compelling leader who builds alliances is the idea of productive cognitive conflict. In essence, this means honest differences of opinion or points of view between earnest people making a good-faith effort to reach the best outcome. In this context, respectfully exploring and explaining areas of disagreement is usually a net positive, in that it allows all those in the meeting to benefit from a perspective they might not encounter otherwise. Good things often follow.

Nonverbal Communication

Overall, the content of your executive interactions as a leader, including ideas exchanged and points made, is crucial. But as a compelling leader, your presentation and approach are also key in interactions, because they help determine how you are perceived by C-suite peers.

Qualities like demeanor, attitude, and personal approach are part of what some experts call executive presence.

As a leader, everything you say matters, but nonverbal communication is also important. For example, one study has found that in spoken in-person communication, 7 percent of meaning comes from the content of words, 38 percent from the speaker's tone of voice – and 55 percent from nonverbal communication. In the workplace, this means that many people make snap decisions about you and your leadership that are largely out of your control.

Given this, as a compelling leader, you should take time to be intentional. This means you should think about what you want to look like, sound like, and stand for as a leader, along the lines of: How do I want to show up as a leader?

In general, self-awareness starts inside and moves outside. It is not always easy, as you may encounter traits about yourself that you discover need adjustment. But knowing and being who you are is a key principle in building executive allies.

One you know this, you can strive to be your best self by making self-improvements, while remaining true to your personality, character, vocabulary, and spirit. In this way, you will be authentic and aspirational, a leader who always aspires to be better through fine-tuning.

In the self-development process, it is often helpful to identify behaviors from role models and other successful leaders that resonate with you, as well as behaviors you would like to avoid. The point here is not to blindly imitate, but to recognize how these leader role models are successful – how they engage, how they communicate, how they carry themselves – and use it to make subtle shifts in your own behavior.

Born or Made?

There's a common debate in leadership circles which centers around a subject that frequently comes up whenever the concept of compelling leadership is discussed: are true leaders born or made?

Likely it is a combination of both. Often, leaders are born with enough empathy and emotional intelligence to be a compelling leader people want to follow, but they are also made by their experiences and by learning what works and what does not.

In addition, compelling leaders are usually acutely aware of their surroundings, and this awareness means they are open to educational or career opportunities that will help them develop. This allows them to charge into circumstances primed for their success.

But if an organization is suffering from a dearth of compelling leaders, it does not mean that those in leadership positions were not born with "the right stuff."

Instead, it is more likely that those leaders are effective managers who got promoted and are not making the effort to develop into compelling leaders. Many managers are promoted for performance in a professional function, and not for their ability to lead people. Often those leadership traits are never developed: they are not willing to make changes and adjustments, and sometimes they do not care enough about the people they lead.

But while the common complaint of "there are so few true leaders anymore" is still often heard, there's also reason for optimism regarding the future of leadership. Many, if not most, professionals want to work for compelling leaders, and that desire drives a demand that never diminishes. In many organizations, team members are ready to give 110% for leaders whom they trust and respect, and who value them as an associate.

That demand means opportunity for you. Even if you were not born with exceptional abilities, you can become a compelling leader if you put in the time and effort to develop the right internal assets, and lead not only with your head but with your heart. For in the end, it is all about how you make them feel.

18

LESSONS FROM POLITICAL LEADERSHIP: WHEN THE UNIMAGINABLE IS REAL

Here in the United States, many dramatic leadership episodes have played out on the public stage in the last few decades. Some seem, in retrospect, like morality plays, holding lessons for leaders of all stripes.

In a previous chapter on crisis leadership, I discussed two events I covered as a reporter that demonstrated the risk of inadequate crisis preparation and insufficient after-crisis response.

Here, I will briefly recount two more dramatic events that demonstrated another hazard of leadership – the consequences, sometimes deadly, of a leadership vacuum.

Chaos under Blue Skies

Tuesday dawned mild in Washington on September 11, 2001, and the morning soon turned exquisite. The sky was cloudless and extraordinarily blue. The usual harsh humidity and haze, common at that time of year, never materialized, and by early morning the temperature hit a gloriously comfortable 70.

I was working a 10–6 shift that day as a correspondent for a global wire service. In those days my morning routine was accompanied by music, never television, but for some reason that day before leaving my apartment I decided to flip on the TV.

A horrific image immediately came into view: an airliner crashed into the North Tower of the World Trade Center in New York City. Shocked, I assumed I would be writing about a catastrophic accident that morning, and I quickly headed out the door.

This was the pre-smart phone era, so people were not wired with breaking news at their fingertips. As I rode the metro reading the *Washington Post* (the actual paper version), I had no idea that a second airliner was then crashing into the South Tower, and that both crashes were in actuality terrorist attacks.

When I left the metro station at about 9:45 a.m., downtown seemed quietly abuzz in an almost imperceptible way. Some pedestrians seemed to be striding quicker than usual, and there was a faint sense of agitation in the air. I was walking to my office near the National Press Building when I overheard someone say, *The Pentagon was hit.*

That phrase, in tandem with the slightly-off feel of downtown, suggested that the incident in New York was no accident. Before I reached my office I saw our U.S. Treasury correspondent hurrying up the street, and he confirmed my suspicion.

Then I noticed a police officer attempting to clear people off the sidewalk on 14th Street, just outside of my office. I asked him the reason for the clearance, and he calmly told me that the FBI said another plane seemed to be headed for the White House (four blocks away), and they were charged with clearing away people who might be in that plane's path.

I arrived to a newsroom in chaos. A flurry of reports flashed over the networks, cable stations, and other wires. The fourth plane was headed for the U.S. Capitol. The National Mall was reportedly on fire. There was a car bomb explosion outside the State Department. Another explosion was reported in the residential section of Capitol Hill. When that last report flashed over the television, one of my female coworkers screamed and started crying. She lived in that area of the Hill, and her husband and child were home that morning.

Three Hours of Hell

Adding to this chaos and uncertainly was a leadership vacuum at the top.

At about 9:30 a.m., President Bush made a short televised public statement from the elementary school in Florida at which he had been visiting for an education-related event. He spoke briefly in front of an audience of about 200 teachers and students at the school. "Today, we've had a national tragedy," Bush said, and then briefly described the World Trade Center crashes as "an apparent terrorist attack on our country."

But the brief report Bush gave was fragmentary. It did not mention what seemed to be in progress after the WTC was hit, and what might still be out there. Bush also said he was returning to Washington, but from that point on he seemed to disappear off the radar for about three hours.

Those three hours were among the most distressing and confusing in modern U.S. history. National news broadcasts reported that casualties in New York City were in the thousands. There were reports that six planes had been hijacked, and three were still at large. Other reports claimed that the WTC and Pentagon attacks were the first wave of a multiple wave attack operation.

The attacks were so unprecedented that there seemed to be no reference point or previous experience to serve as context and guidance on how to proceed. Would there be more attacks? Would other facilities be bombed or blown up? Should those in big cities and near national landmarks take shelter? Where were the safe places? In the middle of an unprecedented attack, had the president gone into hiding? How would the country proceed?

These questions all went unanswered in the leadership vacuum. No official word came from the government. "Where is the president of the United States?" ABC news anchor Peter Jennings said during his network's live broadcast that morning.

As it happened, President Bush recorded a short two-minute statement from a military base in Louisiana, and his remarks were broadcast on television a little after 1 p.m. ET, breaking the three-hour silence at the top. But the brief remarks seemed halting and far short of what the moment required.

The president looked uncertain and nervous. He stumbled over several phrases, his remarks contained few key details, and the statements bordered on the platitudinous. "We have taken all appropriate security precautions to protect the American people." "We have taken the necessary security precautions to continue the functions of your government." "We have been in touch with leaders of Congress and with world leaders to assure them that we will do whatever is necessary to protect America and Americans."

President Bush did not arrive back in Washington D.C. until almost 7 p.m., and he did not make an address to the waiting nation from the White House until 8:30 p.m.

Lessons for Leaders

Few if any current leaders at any organizational level will face a crisis of the magnitude that President Bush faced on 9/11. Nonetheless, the lessons for leaders of all types were several.

One is that when a crisis hits, a full day's absence, with little or no information from executive leadership, is disastrous for an organization.

Another is the importance of presentation and composure during a crisis. President Bush's first public statement came from Florida right after he heard the news of the attack. But Bush's second statement was recorded three hours later – long enough of an interval, even during a crisis, to regain composure and ensure that his delivery and demeanor would be composed and confident. Instead, Bush seemed unsure and halting, and like he was reading (and occasionally misreading) a set of instructions provided to him. He was not the resolute face of the nation.

Another lesson is the cost of making statements about key matters that turn out to be questionable. In his first statement at 9:30 a.m. from Florida, Bush said publicly that he would be returning to Washington. The implication was that his return would be immediate, and that he would be back at the White House within a few hours. But at around 1:30 p.m., Bush was seen on television making a statement from Louisiana, with no mention of Washington.

The price paid for this questionable statement and late arrival was that it sent the wrong message: When America was attacked, the nation's top leader went on the run.

Finally, the episode held a lesson about decision-making. In this case, it involved the importance of clarity regarding the leader's authority and who makes what calls.

The Secret Service, represented by the Air Force One pilot, decided to keep President Bush away from Washington because of the possibility of further attacks. Bush argued against this action, but then relented and allowed stops in Louisiana and the U.S. Command Center in Nebraska, before finally insisting he be flown back to D.C.

This raises the question – who exactly makes the final call here? Was Bush overstepping presidential authority, or should he have made the call to return that morning?

This is a key point for leaders to consider. Decision-making responsibility, and the advise-and-consent process, should be clear in an organization – especially in times of crisis.

An Extended Vacuum

Nearly two decades later, another U.S. leadership vacuum occurred, but this one with far deadlier consequences.

When COVID-19 came to the United States in early 2020, President Donald Trump decided to maintain the public posture of: Everything's under control. As Trump later told the *Washington Post* reporter Bob Woodward, he decided not to tell the American people that the novel coronavirus was a deadly airborne virus far worse than the flu, so as not to set off a panic.

When the virus started rapidly spreading, the Trump Administration took a few actions, such as implementing some restrictions on flights from China and forming a task force of experts that drafted some public guidelines.

But for the most part, there was no robust response to the crisis from the Trump Administration.

Some governors attempted to fill the vacuum in their own states with an active response, but Trump sometimes muddied the prevention message with his demonstrated disdain for masks and social distancing, and his boldness in holding unmasked events.

Overall, Trump did not lead the country's preventive response, but criticized the response of others, such as certain governors. Many found this unprecedented – an abdication of federal leadership in the face of a massive national crisis. A report from Columbia University found this inaction to be deadly.

"Through comparative analysis and applying proportional mortality rates, we estimate that at least 130,000 deaths and perhaps as many as 210,000 could have been avoided with earlier policy interventions and more robust federal coordination and leadership," the report found. In March 2021, Dr. Deborah Birx, the Administration's coronavirus response coordinator, said in a CNN documentary that she thought close to 400,000 deaths could have been avoided with a more effective response.

For leaders, this episode has been a stark lesson of the consequences of insufficient leadership and inadequate crisis response. The scope of the tragedy was unreal. One day in early December 2020, COVID deaths exceeded 3,000 in a 24-hour period – more than the 2,977 Americans killed on 9/11.

PART IV
LEADERS IN ACTION

19
CASE STUDY #1: LEADERSHIP AND VALUES IN SILICON VALLEY

CAROLINE WONG

Fridays are traditionally dress-down days, pandemic notwithstanding. But at one of my early jobs, the last day of the week brought Baileys Irish Cream in the morning coffee and mimosas for all staff.

At company parties, executives ferried around trays of vodka shots. No, these execs were not exactly greed-is-good Gordon Gekko acolytes, nor were they the hedonist Wolves of Wall Street. But they were, in fact, something of a West Coast version of these folks: the Coyotes of Silicon Valley.

I was a young woman – naïve, but sharp and ambitious – and I was in tech. LinkedIn had just gone public and taken off like a rocket, and we were sure to be the next stratospheric IPO. I was in it for the experience, the glitz and the glam, and, yes, the money.

Pressure was also part of the program, so I did feel a bit better after a drink. Then one drink became two drinks…and two became five. The booze, the lunches, the swag – this was all to build a sense of entitlement but also a feeling of compulsion, and of conspiracy. Whatever the jig was, staff were in on it, and we were along for the ride.

Except that this was not a merry band of work hard/play hard young techies all moving toward an ambitious shared goal. Here, abuse, nastiness, and staged internal competitions were all an integral part of the culture.

Let's call the company Tantalize.Tech (not its real name). At Tantalize, the tech titans were brilliant jerks. To be sure, they had plenty of role models in our industry. But here, that ethos was adopted as a requirement: being brilliant in the Valley meant you <u>had</u> to be a jerk. It was not just accepted, but expected.

It's a management approach based on a premise of scarcity: talent is limited, so the top guys (always guys) are kings, with the rest of the organization built to serve them. I was on the information security management team, reporting to the CISO. My experience was a microcosm of the overall management culture, and of the overarching unreality of the enterprise itself.

At the hands of two male colleagues, I faced continual bullying and harassment. (Another aspect of scarcity: If the sun shines on a colleague, that means less light for you.) Rather than rebel, I endured. I numbed myself against the bullying with alcohol. I even found myself adopting the prevailing sense of entitlement: If my brand of flavored water had not been restocked in the company fridge in the morning, I would be grumpy all day.

I stayed on for awhile, confident as we all were that the payout would be worth it. But I eventually discovered that I could endure only so much.

The Goodbye Touch

The last straw came when two colleagues orchestrated a management team meeting with the sole aim of making me look incompetent. I had already been through a lot by then, and this seemed a bridge too far.

Even worse, I saw there was no way to raise my concerns. Had I been more confident, perhaps I would have filed a formal complaint, spoken with colleagues, adopted a wellness regime, talked to a therapist, allowed myself to cry. I did none of those things.

I did identify one C-level exec I was sure would be sympathetic. She was the senior-most woman in the company. She was a bit alternative in her style, and I thought surely she would hear me out. But my entreaty was met with not much more than a shrug, and it was evident that she was not going to rock the boat on my behalf. She was one of them, and I was not.

I exited rather painlessly. I had my share of scars; amid the abuse, I had also been disoriented by a bout of alcoholism – an exceedingly negative experience, one that would take me years to fully crack. But I still had some excellent connections from a previous job, and so a former colleague now working at a truly outstanding company lured me away for a great new position with significant managerial responsibilities.

I give my two-week notice and then, by consent, left in one day. At the very last moment in the office, one of my colleagues snuck in a final grope. Just gross. But HR shuffled me some extra share options as I walked out the door, and off I went.

A Personal Credo

As it happened, corporate leadership later found out that if being brilliant meant you were also a jerk, being a jerk was no guarantee that you were brilliant. The Tantalize IPO, when it arrived, was a dud. The modest opening price immediately tanked (a decade later, it has still not climbed back). The business model was simply not there, and as the market quickly assessed, these emperors had no clothes.

Fortunately, I was gone by then, and I never looked back. This is the first time I have spoken publicly about the whole experience.

I realize now that the value I gained from that painful period has been far richer than those options (which later turned practically worthless anyway). It seared into me some vital lessons about my own employment and my own philosophy as a leader now that I am a C-level executive.

As a young employee, it had never occurred to me to consider the decency of upper management and peers. How could you even gauge that in an interview? Besides, I always found people to be generally good, and I expected work colleagues to be kind and supportive.

In this my perspective may have been distorted by the nurturing experience I had at my first job at eBay. My boss Dave Cullinane treated me with tremendous respect and trusted me with responsibilities well above my level. His support was so important to me, I dedicated my first book (*Security Metrics: A Beginner's Guide*) to him.

After my time at Tantalize, I committed to assessing a company's culture and its people when considering employment there. Decency, respect, and trust have now become my non-negotiables. Unless leadership is committed to these values, I will not cross the threshold.

I will never again work at a place where I don't feel psychologically safe or respected. It's a shame to have to focus on a principle that should be a given. But it's not, and since establishing this as my own personal credo, all my career experiences have been rewarding and fulfilling. This approach led me directly to the position I have today.

Cobalt's Core Values

Throughout my career, I have often reflected on my days at Tantalize. In the job I held after that, I managed five experienced staff, all men, some decades senior to me, and we established an open, mutually supportive, and respectful rapport. I loved the challenge. We all worked hard alongside each other; but for some continuing corporate changes, I might have stayed put.

By the time I came to look for my current position, I had a track record at several major tech firms and was well-established in the infosec community. I was spoiled for choice, with the luxury of interviewing at 15 different companies.

Of these, I chose the smallest and earliest stage. Cobalt.io employed no more than ten people, all working from a converted apartment in the Mission district of San Francisco, with four Danish founders. I was offered a vital role as Vice President for Security Strategy, to help the company revolutionize penetration testing through an innovative approach called Pentesting as a Service (PtaaS). It was a no-name venture where the cofounders restocked the toilet paper and took out the trash.

Why opt for such uncertainty? Core values. I could see the founders had values matching my own. First, they were committed to the work, and to building the company, not fantasizing about a quick filthy rich exit. Second, they were committed to people. Yes, they had Big Ideas, but they were convinced that the only way to build it was with a great team. Lastly, they were committed to a culture of openness.

I believe that, without my experience at Tantalize, I might not have made such a bold choice based on alignment with personal values.

Transparent, Supportive, Celebratory

Four years on, I now serve as Chief Strategy Officer and Head of People at Cobalt. That is, I lead IT/security *and* personnel.

Cobalt has grown to a staff of more than 150, and in summer 2020, we secured Series B (i.e., second-round investment) funding to the tune of $29 million. While establishing and growing an industry-renowned community of talented hackers, I relocated smoothly (pre-pandemic) from the San Francisco area to Portland, Oregon, and am enjoying very active parenting with my husband and two children.

Cobalt maintains extremely high standards for our teams. We have to work at a world-class level. So, how do we do it?

At the heart of our success is a corporate culture based on human values. This is led by our founders, and it is no coincidence that they bring European social principles to a hard-driving Silicon Valley enterprise. When Cobalt CEO Jacob Hansen appointed me Head of People, he explained that he wanted me to ensure that we are always supporting and investing in our staff. To attract, acquire, and retain great talent, we need to build an environment that cultivates personal and professional performance, growth, and happiness.

Taking up this challenge, and working at Jacob's direction, I have highlighted three principles:

1. Radical transparency
2. Celebrating staff
3. Supporting people

The first component of this management philosophy, and my personal starting point, is radical transparency. Of course, we do not share personnel, salary, or client records, and as an infosec firm, we ensure that confidential operational information is secure. (Yes, we pentest ourselves all the time.)

But every other shred of corporate, strategic, planning, and financial information is made fully available, from board decks to monthly departmental results to our cash position. We believe that this shows respect. That we have nothing to hide. And that it helps everyone understand day-to-day business decisions. If we don't have the money for something, everyone can see it for themselves in black and white.

This transparency is also collaborative. We hold two all-hands meetings each month, with the second serving as an open forum to address any and all questions. Staff can submit anonymous queries, and executives stay on the line to answer every last one.

A Slack channel, dubbed "One More Thing," is open to anyone to put forward additional questions. No surprise, one question we get from time to time is about our exit strategy (Will we IPO? Be acquired? What's our timeline?). The honest reply is that we have no current plans. But no questions, including this key issue, are out of bounds. When we secured our latest funding round, we told staff ten days before the public announcement – an unusual approach but a sign of trust and respect.

Second, we believe in celebrating our staff. When we can (that is, pandemic aside), we bring the team together for a kickoff meeting.

Through these events, we developed corporate values. Mission statements often tend toward the anodyne. Ours, however, involves active engagement by the entire company. The value statements are focused and specific:

1. *Humble Learning*. We all learn all the time. We learn from success, and from failure. The CEO learns from the most junior hire. We learn from reading; the company pays for any

book bought by a staff member, as long as they read it and post a short review.

2. *Lead with Grit.* We work through challenges. We do the boring bits as well as the exciting stuff. Everyone, from leadership on down, pitches in. We get the job done.

3. *Quality at Speed.* Infosec is time-sensitive, and we are determined to deliver without ever compromising quality. We recognize that this means prioritizing, not demanding everything at once. So, we make choices, and we focus.

4. *One Cobalt.* We believe that, at our best, $2+2=10$. Teams cooperate, within groups and across the company – sharing, helping, everyone pulling together. Achievements are recognized, but in the end credit belongs to the team as a whole.

To highlight these concepts and their meaning, we award staff members for outstanding representations of these values. The events are often quite emotional. Individuals are celebrated, and colleagues come forward to give praise. These moments make our globally dispersed company into a true community.

Better Than Vodka

Third, we work on the basis of trust and support our staff as people. I can best explain this through my own experience.

When I started at Cobalt, my first child was only a year old. I was constantly juggling childcare and personal commitments. At one point, I mentioned that I rescheduled a nonurgent doctor's appointment to attend a sales call. The CEO replied, "Caroline, I never want you to do that again. Your family and your health come first. There will be thousands of sales calls."

As a young mother, it made a strong impression on me. It was backed up with flexible hours and, a decade before the COVID-19 pandemic, working from home when needed. When I became pregnant with my second child, I was hoping for the statutory minimum of six weeks "disability" pay, even though as a small company we were not bound by that.

The response? Leadership provided 13 weeks of fully paid parental leave, regardless of the details of the type of childbirth. I was welcome to stay on leave as long as I wished beyond that. During that time, two of the founders visited me at home, leaving a thoughtful gift for the baby.

When I returned, rather than making me feel guilty for an extended absence, they gave me a promotion and a raise. Later, my move to the Pacific Northwest was readily accommodated. When a family illness compelled me to abruptly skip out of a critical industry conference, our CEO told me not to worry, and graciously undertook my presentations in my stead.

I did not receive this kind of personal support because of my seniority. I do like to think my dedication was a factor – show commitment to the company, and they will show it back. But more important, it is a central part of our culture. And as the company has grown to more than 100 people, it is now codified in our company policies.

These policies include a number of "appreciation" perks: a reward when people reach their second anniversary, an open invitation to cover the cost of a meal with visiting colleagues. We are especially proud of our Emotional Assistance Program (EAP), which has been popular during the pandemic. Through the EAP, support is made available to any staff member to help manage any personal problem – whether it be online therapy, a home meal service for an elderly parent, or anything else causing stress.

Our approach also includes several feedback mechanisms. There will always be questions and strains, even among high-functioning individuals. Staff can be satisfied and stressed at the same time. We have a 94 percent participation rate in our monthly satisfaction surveys, and leadership reads the responses obsessively to address all the issues.

At Cobalt, we are convinced that the way to get the best out of people is to ensure that they are as happy as possible in their personal lives. People are not machines, and life has all kinds of ups and downs. We have found that if you support staff and show them trust, they will give back with a full heart.

As a parent, I like to think we are a great place for employees with families. For my part, because of this care and attention, I am passionate and devoted in my loyalty to the company – much more than I ever was downing vodka shots.

Making Values Our Business

I should emphasize that all this is based on high professional standards. When necessary, we terminate underperforming staff members as quickly as possible. Bad apples can have a very damaging impact, not only on results but on morale.

I always come back to these basic questions for any manager: Why hire employees if you do not value them? Why oversee staff if you do not support them to do their best? In our high-tech, innovation-led, hyper-competitive age, how can you not listen to and encourage staff members and empower teams, and not maximize the benefits they generate?

As part of performance evaluations, we create a specific personal development plan for each staff member. Rather than denigrating employees and keeping them in a box, I want my staff to be smarter than me – always growing, always pushing me.

These policies and the broader, enabling corporate culture that sustains them all arise from the company's core human values. In my days at Tantalize.Tech, I saw a different way to run a business. I experienced a toxic workplace filled with fear and mistrust, competition, and negativity. I know firsthand not just how painful that is, but also how ineffective as a business model. So again, I will only work for a company that shares my values. And once on board, I will do everything I can to strengthen and spread those values.

At Cobalt.io, we are still in the early stages of growing our business and deepening our values. But I can tell you with absolute certainty that the two go hand in hand.

Caroline Wong is Chief Strategy Officer at Cobalt.io. Her broad infosec experience in Silicon Valley includes tenures as a Cigital consultant, a Symantec product manager, and day-to-day leadership roles at eBay. She is author of the popular textbook Security Metrics: A Beginner's Guide, *and creator of the podcast* Humans of Infosec.

20

CASE STUDY #2: CISO vs. CSO: THE VIEW FROM WEST AFRICA

MCLEAN ESSIENE

Security leadership and management are both part of the interwoven tapestry of an organization, and they can be thought of as threads running through different sections of the fabric, including the risk management and profit-generating sections. But they are distinct threads, each with their own shade.

This distinction is illustrated well by Abraham Zaleznik's seminal *Harvard Business Review* article from 1977, *Managers and Leaders: Are They Different?* Zaleznik argued that managerial function at the time focused solely on building competence, control, and the appropriate balance of power. But this list of actions, he explained, omits the essential leadership elements of inspiration, vision, and human passion – which drive corporate success.

Zaleznik further advanced the contrast as follows. Managers embrace processes, seek stability and control, and instinctively try to resolve problems quickly. Leaders, on the other hand, tolerate chaos and lack of structure, and are willing to delay closure to understand the issues more fully.

As a professional in the security industry based in Nigeria, I have experience in the public, private, and corporate sectors as both a manager and a leader. I have found that the typical security management function is rule-based and profitability-driven, while typical security leadership is people-centered and sustainability-driven.

This implies that while a leader is an effective and influential manager, a manager is not always an effective leader. Despite the distinction, organizations need both functions to succeed.

Leading and Managing in Corporate Security

I have a mixed corporate background. I have worked in a small national company, as well as with a large multinational oil and gas corporation. Each organization had its unique complexities and challenges that I had to navigate to meet business objectives.

From my experience, I learned that two major factors have a profound influence on security management and leadership styles: the size and maturity level of organizations. For example, the majority of domestic firms here in West Africa are medium- to small-sized, and their ESRM maturity level can be described as "repeatable to ad hoc."

Multinational corporations, in contrast, have optimized processes with a matrix leadership structure of different disciplines and teams with enough diverse skills and expertise to tackle specific business challenges.

These factors influence the effectiveness of the respective security programs. In each case, I strived to appreciate realities on the ground to stay flexible and lead effectively.

In the multinational corporation, I served in a supervisory role directly responsible for high-level intelligence analysis to identify trends and threats that could impact the company's assets and operations within my areas of operational jurisdiction. I was involved in the daily intelligence process, and provided timely tactical and strategic support for the company's operations in a VUCAH (volatile, uncertain, complex, ambiguous, and hyper-connected) threat landscape.

In this highly volatile environment, to effectively coordinate activities in a diverse workplace comprising different government security agencies, civilian staff, and vendors required emotional intelligence and systemic thinking competencies. It also involved strong communication skills, in order to maintain mutually beneficial relationships.

This complex, dynamic, and constantly evolving threat landscape stretched the delicate balance between management and leadership until I put on my "systemic thinking cap." Akin to adopting a three-dimensional mindset, it allowed me to quickly synthesize the interconnectedness of events and efficiently manage feedback in providing leadership.

One related leadership achievement for me here was to lead a handful of military personnel members into joining a security industry association, ASIS International, and giving follow-up support in their efforts to achieve certification. These members now have ongoing support as they transition into private sector security.

CISO Leadership Amid Small Organization Challenges

In the small national company I worked with, security struggled to gain recognition and stay visible. This led to funding shortfalls for the security department; company leaders viewed security as a cost center as opposed to an essential business unit. Sometimes this challenge was exacerbated by the inability of those representing the security department to speak the language of business.

Corporate governance was sometimes lacking in some areas, including structures to manage oversight for information risk management, enterprise architecture, and business continuity. In this case, I served in the role of CISO to lead information security governance. I monitored the major drivers and business enablers, including regulatory compliance, organizational alignments, and privacy. Although information security disciplines are technically diverse, I had the core competencies to provide the required level of leadership.

I intended to utilize the ISO 27005 Risk Management frameworks to set up a program and build the information portfolio and security operation. However, the proposal suffered a blow from management; there was insufficient buy-in due to the lack of corporate governance structure and leadership interest.

The organization was vulnerable to a cyberattack with a mere reliance on VPNs and firewalls without robust network incident response and management policy. Shortly after, there were reports of cyber breaches and data losses. Yet, security leaders bore part of the blame for the breaches despite having communicated risk and demonstrated security's value.

Leadership as a CEO

As the CEO of a small private security company, ESSIMACS International Security Ltd. (EISL), and with a team of 12 permanent staff nationwide, I spend a typical day wearing multiple hats: providing leadership to the team, attending to a client, and devoting time to volunteer roles at different industry associations. EISL is a retail loss prevention business, also involved in corporate security management consultancy. Though we are yet a small company, we are strategic in dealing with our clients and business partners.

Available data shows that security management is largely a second-career for most professionals and a dump for military and law enforcement retirees, leading to a wide generational gap between the veterans and young professionals. Therefore, in the private arena within my team at EISL, I wear both hats of an effective manager and a security leader. I also lead the somewhat contrasting functions of driving profitability and sustainability, concurrently.

Here, one must become a flexible workplace coach and a utility infielder while driving business targets. This approach is crucial because the only key to a sustainable security industry is to (like football clubs) develop "feeder teams" for succession while pursuing business goals. This is the core of leadership: developing people for growth. As the Singapore Institute of Management (SIM) encourages, the focus is on performance development rather than performance management.

At the peak of the economic recession in Nigeria in 2016, and then again early in 2020 in the middle of the COVID-19 lockdown, downsizing was imminent and seemed the only plausible option to remain in business. However, as a leader with a focus on strong employee relationships, we were able to work out a less stringent cost-cutting strategy. Rather than severing some staffers, we instead settled for proportionate wage reductions across the board so everyone earns a little less but happily so, as they kept their positions.

To develop talent and nurture succession, I empower subordinates and increase efficiency by delegating responsibility. We also influence and enhance professionalism by tying specific roles and promotions to top industry credentials such as those delivered by ASIS, IFPO, and the Loss Prevention Foundation. For instance, for a supervisory role, a CPO credential is a minimum requirement. We continually inspire our teams to achieve success.

Management and leadership have increasingly become strategically organic. I also provide oversight leadership for clients and subtly influence their organizational culture. For our retail and wholesaler clients, for instance, we encourage profitability by rigorously striving to embed loss prevention procedures and enforce compliance in their operations, to curtail theft and shrink. We place the customer at the center of our business model.

The Blurred CISO/CSO Line

Due to budgetary limitations, small companies often have a high risk of staff turnover due to inadequate resources and inability to sustain and develop the right talent required for strategic growth. Other common challenges are a lack of business continuity and contingency plans in place and a lack of established information security governance.

Sometimes there is a blurred line between the roles of the CISO and the CSO in a small organization. One way to gain visibility, and to adapt to the blurred roles of physical and information security disciplines, is to implement enterprise security risk management and to place enterprise-wide security risks in a single risk portfolio open to collaborative influence across the organization.

To continue to make progress in an increasingly VUCAH business environment, security managers and leaders must constantly broaden their strategic perspectives and seek innovative ways of dealing with challenges. Regardless of the management and leadership style and the nomenclature used, leaders and managers should be change-ready and be able to quickly and skillfully navigate complexities and deal with new realities, to remain aligned with organization's purpose and strategy.

With the present coronavirus pandemic new normal and a future of macro uncertainties, effective security management and leadership will become increasingly essential not only for business success but also to rebuild better. Be it in big or small organizations, security managers must be strategic leaders, who go beyond simply meeting business objectives as they develop into future industry leaders. This, essentially, is how we will lead the future.

McLean Essiene, CPP, PCI, PSP, is a seasoned security management consultant and trainer in Nigeria. He has worked for the Nigeria Immigration Service and in private security with both a multinational company and a local security firm. In 2019, he won an Outstanding Security Performance Award (OSPA) as the Nigeria Outstanding Young Security Professional.

21
CASE STUDY #3: REDEFINING LEADERSHIP DURING THE 2020 PANDEMIC

CHRIS STUART

What is leadership? If you had asked me prior to March 2020, I would have replied that leadership was a lofty concept that one learns about, at least in part, through books written by experienced CEOs and webinars presented by senior managers who are skilled at inspiring their teams to achieve a common goal.

But then came the great equalizer known as the coronavirus. Suddenly there were no books, no webinars, no instruction manuals with tried-and-true advice on how to effortlessly navigate the crisis that our nation, and our nation's industries, were facing when life as we knew it changed dramatically in the first quarter of 2020. Within days, company executives were forced to redefine what it means to be an effective leader during a time of great uncertainty that is still evolving.

When the first cases of COVID-19 in the United States were diagnosed in a nursing home located in Washington State, it was generally understood that we were racing towards the unprecedented. At Top Guard Security, our regional family-owned private security services firm, we were not immune from the severe impact of the virus on our business and our clients. In fact, the pandemic challenged us to open new pathways for providing exceptional services to our clientele. I found myself leading those initiatives in ways not previously imagined.

But first, let me give you some background on pre-COVID life at Top Guard. As the Vice President of Top Guard Security, I'm responsible for business development, contract negotiations, and anything remotely related to marketing. The firm was founded by my wife, Nicole, and has steadily grown in revenue and staff for 24 consecutive years; 2021 marks our milestone 25th anniversary.

Top Guard is now the largest woman-owned employer in the Commonwealth of Virginia.

While Top Guard has thrived since 1996, the pandemic found us searching for advice from specialists and consultants who offered strategies for leading in an environment of paralyzing fear and tremendous uncertainty.

During a podcast at the start of the pandemic, business and entrepreneurship expert Carl Gould recommended: "Tell your staff and your clients what you have done, what you are doing, and what they can count on you to do." Based on his suggestion, an e-blast went out to our entire Constant Contact list with precisely that information by the close of business on that very day.

From that e-blast came a reply from one of our industry's most noted advisers, complimenting us on being ahead of the challenge posed by the virus. He asked for permission to reference us in an article he was working on for an industry magazine, and we agreed. The digital article came out a few days later, which led to another e-blast from Top Guard with a link to the article. We've been building on that momentum ever since.

Managing a COVID-Related Assignment and the HIPAA Factor

Our first inquiry driven solely by a need to protect residents from the virus came from a proactive senior care facility in our region. The client had utilized our firm in the past for special events, but had its own in-house or proprietary security team for all other purposes. The comfort level between our two firms was high. The mandate was clear from the manager: "No one is going to lose their life here on my watch." This was a mission that Top Guard could support.

The facility had a number of services that needed to be eliminated for an indefinite period of time. For example, a Welcome Center was to become a We Are Closed to the Public Center, and all incoming staff had to be temperature-scanned. Given the many unknowns so early in the pandemic, the hourly service rate that I quoted was a bit on the high side, to put it mildly. They politely said they would consider it and we didn't hear anything back. However, by the end of the week, they reached out because the healthcare screening firm they hired had severely disappointed them from the start. We began providing security and temperature scanning services at several posts a few days later and were off to the races.

I would like to share a few insights regarding temperature scans. Prior to launching our full-blown temperature scanning services, we followed one of our basic business principles – it is better to invest a little bit upfront for good advice than to make a huge, preventable, and expensive error later. Calls went out to both our business attorney and our human resources attorney.

Their advice was sound and invaluable. First of all, they informed us that Top Guard's security staff members were legally able to conduct temperature scans because a scanning does not require a certification, given that scans do not break the skin nor involve bodily fluids. The second takeaway was that we needed to ensure that individual data attributable to specific persons was not being collected, which could have created a potential Health Insurance Portability and

Accountability Act (HIPAA) violation. Entering such data into any type of electronic device would compound the challenge even further, given the highly sophisticated requirements of HIPAA.

Armed with this intel, I now knew what to ask prospective clients and what to tell them that we could do. Several months into the pandemic, this knowledge again came into play. We encountered a situation where a prospective client very much wanted to create a database of all of the employees' temperature readings. When the human resources director at a heavy industrial manufacturer couldn't be dissuaded from the requirement, we chose to decline the work. In short, a potential disaster was averted from our perspective.

From SOP to Open-Source Solution

Another major contract that we accepted as a result of the virus was diligently building a temporary workforce for the 90-day close down of a large chemical plant. They were shutting everything down to complete a top-to-bottom review.

Our office had hired, processed, and trained 28 full-time workers that would be assigned to the site to supplement the company's regular staff. Their duties were to control access at the numerous entrances and exits that would have to be open to facilitate the vast number of vendors required to complete the process in 90 days. The hiring and training proceeded smoothly and on schedule, so imagine our surprise when the night before we were slated to begin, the client called and informed us that everything was canceled.

The message, in essence, was: "There's no need for the extra staff but thank you for the Herculean effort." We were dumbfounded and, frankly, did not make any executive decisions for two days besides idling the temporary staff because everyone was rendered immobile at having just accomplished this remarkable hiring hurdle, all for naught.

Then, two days after the thanks-but-no-thanks notice, the client called and informed us that they were willing to use the staff we had just hired, but in a slightly different capacity. Were we able to provide temperature scan services at their gates for employees and visitors? "Most certainly!" we quickly replied. We began training and scheduling staff.

After this second client began using our temperature scan services, it dawned on me that we needed to be even more proactive on the temperature scanning front. A quick notice was sent to our director of training: By the time a third client called to inquire about temperature scans, we needed to have a detailed Standard Operating Procedure (SOP) in place.

Our talented team member did not disappoint, and an SOP document was quickly written, designed, and created as a digital document that demonstrated our firm's expertise at this critically needed skill. Our firm was ahead of the curve in this unprecedented time of emergency, and this information was needed. I decided that the most mutually beneficial solution was to spread it far and wide.

Communicating Crucial Health Information

Borrowing a concept from programmers, Top Guard made our Temperature Scanning Best Practices information accessible as an open-source document, customized with our logo and graphics. For distribution, we leveraged many years of working with our regional Chambers of Commerce and professional organizations, which were all of eager for relevant content. They gladly assisted in pushing it out to their members.

I made myself available to ensure that anyone with questions or a specific need could save valuable time by capitalizing on our growing experience with temperature scanning processes and techniques. As a result of our outreach, a new opportunity arose that further enabled our organization to showcase our leadership in this niche expertise area.

The Virginia Manufacturers Association was already providing COVID-19 oriented information to its members weekly. They reached out to Top Guard with a request to create and conduct a webinar for their account management and training development personnel about the temperature scan services that we were providing to several employers of VMA members. During the webinar, we learned that safety professionals were very interested in what was working and what wasn't. They craved information that would support their tremendous responsibilities for keeping essential staff safe and able to work.

Just prior to the VMA webinar, we had started temperature scanning services at a pork processing plant run by a large firm. The firm had suffered some initial setbacks with COVID-19 group infections at other plants across the country, and we were committed to preventing the same scenario from happening in Virginia.

Then came a surprise as the staff received state-of-the-art thermographic camera/computer equipment that had been sent by the company's Chinese owners. At the time, this technology was the envy of everyone. The stark contrast between using hand-held thermometers and James Bond-like thermography was a source of great interest to safety directors scrambling to understand the tools that existed in the marketplace.

The local chapter of ASIS International, a security industry association, learned about our temperature scanning services and asked me to do a webinar. In order to offer maximum value to participants, I expanded the content to include Benjamin Dobrin, Ph.D., a public health professional and dean at Virginia Wesleyan University.

The effect of combining our firm's practical experience with temperature scans with Dr. Dobrin's expertise on public health and COVID-19 issues turned out to be stellar. Participants peppered us with questions that showed just how truly starved they were for useful information in the late spring/early summer of 2020. The event ran over by 20 minutes and the marketer in me concluded that we needed to take this show on the road.

Webinars Prove Effective Outreach Tool

Invitations to present webinars in the Hampton Roads region started filling my calendar. The webinars became an avenue to maximize outreach to prospective clients, and I found myself entering uncharted territory of being a proactive leader in the new normal for safety providers.

For example, I crafted an email that was much more personal in nature than our other e-blasts and sent it to over 100 of my top prospects. Individualized for each recipient, the emails emphasized how Top Guard had stepped into the breach for many essential businesses and stood ready to do so for them. We kept a running total of the number of service hours spent performing temperature scans and included the updated numbers in this correspondence. As of this writing, we currently stand at 100,000+ hours of this specific service – rather impressive given that temperature scanning only began about eight months ago.

Our webinar for the regional Chamber of Commerce had over 100 participants. Dr. Dobrin and I traversed the subject matter quickly, because it was now obvious to us that people wanted ample time for Q&A. Another presentation was for a highly specialized regional task force created to specifically address regionwide virus-related issues in the business community.

The final and most specialized webinars began with a phone call from the executive director of For Kids, a nonprofit dedicated to "breaking the cycle of homelessness and poverty for families & children." The agency had been hard hit by the virus because of mandated shutdowns and a requirement to eliminate interactions between staff and constituents. As a result, families and children that were already suffering from the challenges of homelessness now didn't have access to the many services offered by For Kids.

The director reached out to me when he and his team had designed a plan to be able to provide transportation services again. They had volunteer drivers and ample people in need of the service, but they lacked a template for ensuring that state and federal safety standards were being met. I emailed him our Temperature Scan Best Practices document, yet I had a gnawing feeling that I could do something more.

So I called another friend, the executive director at Volunteer Hampton Roads, an organization dedicated to training nonprofit staff, boards, and volunteers. I described the situation with For Kids and asked if other nonprofits in the region might be facing similar difficulties. The director said they were, and she remarked that few seem to realize that nonprofits need assistance with the same issues that businesses face, but without anywhere near the same resources.

Dr. Dobrin and I were humbled to wrap up our COVID-19 webinar series with a presentation that was custom-designed for the nonprofit community. We both enjoyed assisting local agencies fighting the good fight in times of financial and logistical headaches none of them could have foreseen.

Recognition of Essential Services

In addition to the webinars, an exciting and rewarding leadership opportunity presented itself as the pandemic continued to settle over the nation. The term "essential worker" was newly in vogue, and rightfully so. Our firm was providing security services at facilities of all sizes and temperature scanning at a variety of food manufacturers, food store distribution centers, and other locations that could readily be considered crucial to the American economy. While our academic and municipal clients had trimmed back or eliminated services, the demand for temperature scans and increased security at entrances to businesses and medical facilities rose exponentially.

Security officers in these COVID-era roles were being compensated at special rates, and to recognize their dedication to high-level performance, Top Guard created the "Brass Paw" Award. In an industry that wears uniforms, pins represent an opportunity to recognize accomplishments, such as prior military service, winning an Officer of the Quarter Award, etc.

In the case of the "Brass Paw," any officer that worked temperature scanning shifts, even one, could proudly wear the pin. Chosen in honor of our mascot, an English Bulldog, the "Brass Paw" has become a symbol of pride and reinforces that security providers are one of many industries, such as healthcare, truck drivers, grocery store workers, and others, that have stepped up so selflessly and risen to the occasion during the pandemic of 2020.

In sum, executive leadership challenges are almost impossible to predict, but often present limitless potential. As my role at Top Guard shifted to creating and presenting webinars, distributing "Temperature Scanning Best Practice" content and creating "Brass Paw" awards, I embraced these opportunities to redefine leadership for an already innovative business.

Chris Stuart is Vice President of Top Guard Security, a regional private security services firm headquartered in Norfolk, Virginia. The award-winning firm is the Commonwealth's largest woman-owned employer. He has served on the ASIS International Management and Leadership Council and completed numerous leadership programs. He is Past President of the Virginia Security Association and has served as Chairman of the Board of Directors for several non-profit organizations. He has authored several articles on management and leadership for various publications.

22
CASE STUDY #4: TWO-WAY LEADERSHIP IN ACTION

BILL COTTRINGER

Two-way leadership is a dynamic interactive process, based on a two-way communication model. This model stresses the carpenter's rule of measuring twice and sawing once. The communication equivalent of this is using your two ears to listen twice, and your one mouth to talk once.

Two-way communication helps teach leaders to avoid talking at the other person, in favor of talking with them. This involves active listening to fully understand what is being said, rather than focusing on coming up with a clever response to what you hear. It also involves listening to what is said, how it is said, and what is not said. As the legendary American basketball coach Red Auerbach once said, "It is not what you tell your players that counts, it's what they hear."

Research has found that this type of two-way communication is effective in reducing defensiveness and increasing support, leading to more productive communication outcomes. A defensive climate of communication, according to the sociologist Jack Gibbs, shuts down communication, whereas a supportive climate encourages open communication. This positive climate change involves avoiding attempts at control, manipulation, and judgment, as well as avoiding closed qualities like certainty and superiority.

Instead, open qualities are purposefully conveyed: empathy, acceptance, equality, freedom, and spontaneity. This helps change one-way communication into two-way communications. Both leaders and followers come together as a team that uses a supportive communication style. They openly talk and listen to each other to get a better understanding of the perspectives and details that are involved with the situation at hand.

This situation at hand could be any number of things: a value or personality conflict, a needed organizational change, or a serious productivity problem. Both two-way leadership and two-way communication are founded on people's fundamental needs to be understood, accepted, respected, and valued, and to be reasonably autonomous in having a sense of meaning and purpose in what they are doing.

Below are two case studies involving CSOs which demonstrate the dynamics of two-way leadership in action.

Inclusivity: Friend of Truth

The first case study involves Bob Brickly, a seasoned CSO who is now with a national contract security company on the West Coast of the United States. Bob has mastered the art and science of instructing his supervisors on how to use the two-way leadership model to arrive at the most complete truth of what did or did not happen during an investigation. Investigations had become a big part of his company's business, so there was strong buy-in from upper management to conduct proper and effective ethical investigations. But Bob knew that achieving this required conscientious and diligent effort on the part of the investigators.

Bob had a good track record of successfully resolving difficult "he said-she said" contradictory stories when no independent collaboration was available. In discussion with his supervisors, Bob shared what he knew about people's perceptions being their reality and the faulty ways memory can emotionally wrap perceptions and beliefs into a cement block of certainty. These perceptions and beliefs, he explained, can then become resistant to being changed despite overwhelmingly compelling evidence to the contrary.

Bob firmly believed that exclusivity was the enemy of truth, whereas inclusivity was truth's friend. He lived this value in both his life and work because he understood it to be one of the foundations of two-way communication, which was the best way to get along with others and solve conflicts over what is true or false. He sometimes reminded his team that defensive communication bred exclusivity – picking one side of the equation as okay and the other as not okay – which was the enemy of truth, whereas supportive communication represented the inclusion of both half-truths. Another practical application of this insight Bob used frequently with his team was encouraging team members to figure out a way to say "yes" in an environment that over-protected "no's."

Bob often used examples of his own failure as a good way to begin a difficult discussion of an unpopular idea that was under consideration. After that opening, he went further into the concept of, "much of what we think we know really isn't so." He used the historical example of the lingering belief in the world being flat which severely limited world travel and trade, even after ships first traveled to the anticipated edge and didn't fall off!

Another example Bob used was the traditional concept of time being a measurable mechanical movement from past to present to future. This understanding excluded the psychological version of time being more of an ever-expanding timeless and fluid "now" moment. As explained, the concept turned out to be a game-changer from the perspective of managing time rather than letting it manage the team's efforts in an investigation. Using both perspectives allowed the team's deadlines to be met on time.

With these discussions, Bob's team quickly understood that when two people disagreed as to the events in a situation that was being investigated, the truth usually lies somewhere in between, with some truth and some falsities on both sides. This guideline, of course, had the unspoken caveat that sometimes the truth leaned a little more in the direction of the one rather than the other, all things rarely being equal.

Applying New Understandings to Investigations

With each pending investigation, Bob's teams of investigators (usually with no more than three members) would plan an A-B-C approach, which included the use of two-way leadership and communication, in order to enhance their effectiveness by (a) remembering to be sensitive, be accepting, not be overly serious, be better listeners than talkers, and be approachable; (b) identifying and affirming what corroborative facts were available from independent sources, such as video or audio tapes or eyewitnesses; and then (c) questioning all people involved separately, with oral interviews and follow-up written statements.

After such planning, the challenge moving forward was to clarify the discrepancies in given versions of events to allow for a reasonable conclusion of what most likely happened, given available knowledge. One important point Bob always stressed with his team was to have the tenacity to keep going with the line of questioning they were most likely to give up on, because this often turned out to be the information game-changer. In one unusual investigation of nursing home abuse and theft, the very end of the investigation led to the prosecution of the nursing home manager who had hired Bob's team to do the investigation. Such an outcome was totally unexpected by the team, but without the final finding obtained by tenacious questioning, the investigation would have been a complete failure.

One of the most valuable ways in which Bob helped his team was to aid them in becoming more aware of the effect that their mere presence could have on the investigation outcome. Earlier, Bob had worked out a method of demonstrating how all of us come into a new situation with built-in biases that can alter what we see as the best truth of an event.

To help illustrate the concept of different individual perspectives when looking at something, Bob used a four-sided square box, each side with a different shaped opening – a circle, triangle, square, and rectangle. Each team member sat by one of the four sides and looked at an unknown object that was placed under the box away from view, such as a large rubber toy elephant. Then each of the four lookers reported what they believed to be what they were seeing. Of course, all the responses were different, being influenced by the particular shape of the viewpoint on their side of the box.

Another technique Bob used was designed to demonstrate how tiny changes in language can mean a big difference in meaning. He asked team members to consider the belief that "Peace and happiness can be found *nowhere*" and then changed the wording to "Peace and happiness can be found *now here*." The takeaway: the difference one letter can make in written communication.

One of Bob's more difficult challenges had to do with helping his team understand the human tendency of over-embracing an alluring half-truth that appears to be the full truth. Bob knew this tendency was prevalent and very hard to shake. Nonetheless, he used thoughtful examples and presented them to the team with a supportive tone in two-way communication style. He described the situations in his examples fairly and without judgment. He asked team members if these scenarios could represent half-truths that could be potential problems and what might be some possible solutions, which resulted in many "aha" moments. From there it was not much of a stretch to show how one could question the completeness of a half-truth and not rush to embrace it. The team then explored plausible alternative beliefs to those presented.

Finally, Bob's commitment to continuously improving his practice of two-way leadership led him to an interesting discovery – namely, an intriguing way to increase knowledge in an investigation in the process of closing the gap between what you know and what you need to know to get to the most accurate and complete conclusion. The method involves the "Johari Window," which counselors sometimes use to uncover a patient's blind spot in understanding what they were doing wrong in order to correct the behavior to get where they really wanted to be. Bob thought this concept could be applied to improving the quality of the team's investigations.

Under the Johari Window method, four quadrants are moved through systematically to identify what each party knows and does not know, so that everyone can know more of what is needed to know. In this case, the four quadrants played out for Bob's team as follows.

Quadrant One is what everyone knows, including the team of investigators and the persons being investigated.

Quadrant Two contains what the team knows but the persons being investigated do not know. Quadrant Three is what the persons being investigated know but the investigative team does not know. And finally, Quadrant Four shows what all the players – the investigative team and the persons being investigated – don't know but need to know for proper completion of the investigation.

As it happened, the use of the Johari Window method strengthened Bob's and his team's commitment and practice of two-way communication and leadership, as it allowed the team to critique its own knowledge base and knowledge gaps, instead of a one-way focus on those being investigated. It also helped team members get the best results in the right way, and they went on to become excellent investigators. Finally, it helped them understand that when you use the right means to obtain the right ends, success is virtually guaranteed.

Second Study: Sara's Strategy

The second case study involves Sara Jones, a new CSO for a small proprietary security program in the Midwest of the United States. In her work so far, Sara has been applying an important two-way leadership strategy she learned in her company's orientation training.

This strategy includes using both ways of knowing the truth of something by following both paths of knowledge/reason and feelings/intuition. (Bob used the same strategy in building a better investigation team because it was an effective way for team members to be more aware of eliminating their defensive communication style and replace it with a more supportive approach.)

Sara applied her newly learned two-way leadership strategy to a serious problem her department was having in selecting high-performing and fully engaged officers who wanted a career in security, rather than just a job. What she didn't know at the time was that her company's HR manager was having second thoughts about their established interviewing and selection methods that the company used for replacing retiring employees, as well as younger ones moving on to different career development paths.

Sara first approached her current security officers in small discussion groups to find out two things – what they liked most about the best interview they experienced, and how they would approach a prospective officer they were interviewing. What these current officers said about their best interview validated the basic components of two-way communication and leadership: they all liked interviews that were interactive, where they were understood and accepted for their differences and they thought this was the best way for interviews to be done.

This gave Sara the needed opening to ask her question about how everyone came to this same conclusion. In response, there were looks of uncertainty and hesitation, often present when someone knows the answer to a seemingly rhetorical question, but not how to give it. That silence gave Sara the opportunity to rephrase the question in a way that was more probing. She asked her officers, "How do you know something is certain or not?" Some said, "You have certain feelings or intuitions about it." Others said, "You follow facts and reason to know if it is true." The one officer added, "At any rate, you trust the authority that tells you something is either true or not, whether that authority is your eyes, your mind, or your heart."

From here it was not much of a stretch for Sara to make the connection and use this combination of sound ways to find out if a prospective security officer was a good fit or not.

The team first worked together to develop an application that asked the right questions to obtain essential information. This included the position the person was applying for, contact information, prior work history, references, availability, criminal history related to licensure per state law, education, military service, past training in security, where they found out about the job, understanding of general job duties and requirements, and certifying that all information was accurate.

Next, they organized a structured behavioral interview that measured all the Key Performance Indicators (KPIs), or the combination of knowledge base, abilities, and characteristics that was most inclusive to the profile of successful and satisfied security officers already employed.

This short list included attributes such as honesty, effective communication, coachability, dependability, being cool under pressure, resourcefulness, and having common sense judgment. This new system of security officer selection was successful, and it did not take very long for the company's HR director to find out about it and borrow it from Sara, for companywide application.

Sara's next challenge came with the COVID-19 pandemic. Things quickly changed in her department. There were people calling in and quitting out of fear of exposure to the virus. Duties of the security officers were changing daily. New aspects of training emerged, which she needed to learn about and effectively manage, along with all the other unknowns from the new normal security landscape.

Using two-way leadership, she listened to both her right and left brain in learning all the facts and information she could gather from reading and talking to other managers in her network about where the pandemic was taking everyone, and shared her own thoughts and intuitions with others.

Sara was now experienced enough to know something very important about life and work, which she openly shared with her team: the more you learn about effective problem-solving and conflict resolution, the more difficult the problems and conflicts that confront you are. Life and work have their own ways of testing you. Most of the team members in Sara's group knew this was true from their personal life experiences.

One day Sara received a discrimination complaint from one of her officers about another officer. The situation was a very emotional one for everyone involved, so Sara used both reason and intuitive feelings to discover the truth of the incident to help resolve this conflict before it became a legal matter. When Sara explored both the thinking and feeling of each of the individuals about what was reported, it became apparent that there wasn't any bad intent behind what was said, but the impact landed poorly on the receiver.

Once she had a good understanding of the dynamics of this situation, Sara was able to bring the two officers together to better explain both the rational and emotive aspects of the conflict to them. This took enough sting off of what was said and interpreted to open the door to better two-way communication and better relations between the two officers moving forward. As it turned out, both officers had brought some past emotional experiences to this potentially explosive situation and once that was uncovered, communication was much easier.

Sara doesn't know for sure what her next challenge will be, but one thing she does know is another conflict is just around the bend. She will be prepared in understanding and dealing with it with the two-way leadership style she is committed to because it is in line with a continuous improvement perspective and transferable to a variety of problems and difficult situations.

Maximum Leadership through Championship Teamwork

These two different security managers applied what they knew about two-way leadership and two-way communication in two different settings to get the same result – success.

Success in leadership today comes from leading diverse teams so that team members are unified in purpose and mission. Two-way leadership enables leaders to do this in a way that is more mutually fulfilling, sustaining, and effective than the outdated command-and-control style.

As the best sports teams (with or without an audience present) know, talent wins games, but teamwork wins championships.

William Cottringer, Ph.D., CHS-III, currently serves as Executive Vice President for PalAmerican Security/Cascade Security Corp. He has been involved with the security industry for over 50 years and is a seasoned manager and leader. His professional career started with security police in the U.S.A.F. in 1962 in Japan and Vietnam, and continued into law enforcement, corrections, mental health, university teaching, and private security. He is a regular contributor of leadership articles to Security Management magazine and currently on ASIS International's review committee for its protection of assets project. He has published ten books, available on Amazon.

PART V
THE FUTURE OF MANAGEMENT AND LEADERSHIP

23

MANAGING THE FUTURE, AND LEADING AHEAD OF THE CURVE

Superb management and stellar leadership will be needed more than ever in the future, as an increasing number of hazards will test organizations like never before.

Consider 2020, the year most of this book was written. The COVID-19 public health crisis shook the world up economically, socially, and politically, and added another layer of complication to the many existing global hardships.

The number of people classified under conditions of crisis, emergency, and famine increased in 2020 to almost 135 million people across 55 countries, according to estimates from the United Nations. Meanwhile, a myriad of developments – including the pandemic, military conflicts, economic slowdowns, and natural disasters – have left almost 700 million people undernourished, which equals almost 10 percent of the world's population.

Worldwide challenges and their impacts, such as economic slow-down, political instability, and environmental damage, eventually filter down to societal and organizational levels. Even if your organization has no direct involvement with public health, the global economy, or climate trends, these large-scale developments will translate into factors that affect your firm and the environment in which you work as a manager and leader.

Which managers will thrive in this environment? Those who realize that they can rise to any challenge if they can put the many talents and skills of their teams to best use.

These thriving leaders will manage so that their team members feel enfranchised and empowered, rather than alienated and disengaged.

They will not think of management as a fixed practice, but as an endeavor that demands agility, including the ability to adapt to the evolving values of the workforce and to the ever-shifting environments in which they manage. They will know that they have to be agile to manage their own biases.

They know change is coming, and they expect to be challenged. They have learned to relish the adventure.

Leading Ahead of the Curve

When one looks past the hardship caused by the pandemic and other crises in 2020, a distinct irony comes into view: what if the most serious challenges to management and leadership in the future come out of the unintended consequences of brilliant innovation?

For example, what if artificial intelligence (AI) continues to develop so that, in the words of futurist Scott Klososky, AI goes from "knowing me, to representing me, to being me, to replacing me." Could it cause a mass wipe out of white-collar-sector jobs that has a destabilizing impact on society?

"We invent technologies without ever really having an understanding of what they are going to do to us. It's probably time to get a little wiser," Klososky said at a recent conference I attended.

And what if, as some experts say, current exoskeleton technology evolves into IT implants which augment body processes like brain and organ function. Will these transhuman beings, with their enhanced brains and bodies, use their advantages to become the new elite leaders?

It's likely that we are nowhere near the advanced stages of technological innovation. ("We're five percent into this battle, if that," Klososky said.)

What will this mean for the leaders of the future?

They will understand that as technology continues to advance, the human – which technology can never fully replicate – will become more and more valuable. And so, for all their technical skill, the leaders of the future will be focused on the human side of leadership: forging human connections, facilitating teamwork, and showing that they care about team members.

In hiring and recruiting and promoting, they will look for professionals with key human attributes such as high emotional intelligence, self-awareness, and the ability to think outside the box and question assumptions.

They will recognize, recognize, recognize. Accomplishments by their teams will be frequently articulated. They will offer much more encouragement and praise than criticism.

They will understand that it is very human for people to forget what a leader said or did, yet still remember how that leader made them feel. And so they will help team members feel great, because when the challenges become greater and greater, so does the value of work that meets those challenges.

As mentioned at the beginning of this book, Gallup's recent *State of the Global Workplace* Report contained some grim news for managers: only 21 percent of employees say that their performance is managed in a way that motivates them to do outstanding work. In response, Gallup CEO Jim Clifton set out a charge for leaders worldwide: "Move the world's workplace mission from paycheck to purpose."

The leaders of the future will follow that advice.

Bibliography

Studies

Adaptable Leadership: What It Takes to Be a Quick Change Artist, Center for Creative Leadership.
Crisis Leadership, Center for Creative Leadership.
Culture and Change Management Survey, The Katzenbach Center at PwC.
Onboarding New Employees: Maximizing Success, SHRM Foundation.
Performance Management: The Secret Ingredient, Deloitte.
State of the American Workplace, Gallup.
State of the Global Workplace, Gallup.
What Great Managers Do to Engage Employees, Gallup.
2020 Retention Report, The Work Institute.

Books

Coaching for Results, by Steven J. Stowell/Cherissa S. Newton/Eric D. Mead.
The Coaching Habit, by Michael Bungay Stanier.
Emotional Intelligence: Why It Can Matter More Than IQ, by Daniel Goleman.
The First 90 Days, by Michael Watkins.
Good in a Room, by Stephanie Palmer.
Management Challenges of the 21st Century, by Peter Drucker.

Index

Printed in the United States
by Baker & Taylor Publisher Services